The
Confidence
Effect

Every Woman's Guide to the
Attitude That Attracts Success

GRACE KILLELEA

AMACOM AMERICAN MANAGEMENT ASSOCIATION
New York ◦ Atlanta ◦ Brussels ◦ Chicago ◦ Mexico City
San Francisco ◦ Shanghai ◦ Tokyo ◦ Toronto ◦ Washington, D.C.

This publication is designed to provide accurate and authoritative information in regard to the subject matter covered. It is sold with the understanding that the publisher is not engaged in rendering legal, accounting, or other professional service. If legal advice or other expert assistance is required, the services of a competent professional person should be sought.

Library of Congress Cataloging-in-Publication Data
Killelea, Grace.
The confidence effect : every woman's guide to the attitude that attracts success / Grace Killelea.
    pages cm
Includes bibliographical references and index.
ISBN 978-0-8144-3641-7 (hardcover) — ISBN 0-8144-3641-2 (hardcover) —ISBN 978-0-8144-3642-4 (ebook) 1. Women executives. 2. Women—Employment. 3. Self-confidence. 4. Self-esteem in women. 5. Women—Vocational guidance. 6. Success in business. I. Title.
HD6054.3.K45 2016
658.4'09082—dc23

                                                                    2015022941

About AMA
American Management Association (www.amanet.org) is a world leader in talent development, advancing the skills of individuals to drive business success. Our mission is to support the goals of individuals and organizations through a complete range of products and services, including classroom and virtual seminars, webcasts, webinars, podcasts, conferences, corporate and government solutions, business books and research. AMA's approach to improving performance combines experiential learning—learning through doing—with opportunities for ongoing professional growth at every step of one's career journey.

Printing number
10 9 8 7 6 5 4 3 2

For my mom, Audemia Ozvalda Killelea (Thea), who taught me lessons that have lasted a lifetime. You were the first person to tell me I could do anything and be anything I wanted to be, and with those words you planted a seed of confidence. You left your handprint on my heart.

Contents

Photos of the interviewees in this book can
be found at theconfidenceeffectbook.com.

Preface

Success and happiness are not just for the world's richest, luckiest, thinnest, or smartest women. We can be successful and happy even when we aren't given every opportunity or advantage. I know because I have never been the richest, thinnest, most beautiful, luckiest, or smartest woman in the world. Yet, I've created a life, career, and business that I love—despite significant challenges.

Along the way, I found that the negative voices in my head are lying, and that by connecting my internal knowledge to my external energy—or, simply put, my competence to my confidence—I could achieve both success and happiness. In 2013, at the age of 53, I ended my corporate career as a senior vice president of a Fortune 50 company and launched what has become a premier leadership program for high-potential women. I'm a woman who has been morbidly obese, yet I've walked several 60-mile events and skydived to celebrate losing more than 120 pounds. I survived a devastatingly bad marriage, and at 55, I met and married a wonderful man.

I wrote this book because for many years I was the woman who believed just working hard was "enough." I was the classic "good girl" who said yes to everything I was asked to do at work, yet never asked for anything in return. I was the woman who spent too many years listening to the negative voices inside my head and the ones forced upon me by society.

When I walked into a room, I'd have the "I'm not" conversation in my head. You know how that conversation goes. *I'm not*:

○ *Smart enough*

○ *Thin enough*

○ *Attractive enough*

○ *Experienced enough*

○ *Worthy enough*

○ *Deserving enough*

I was always waiting for building security to come and haul me away—feeling like a fraud, sure I'd be found out—and yet that never happened.

The Confidence Effect is my way to give you shortcuts and provide you with tools to help you connect your confidence to your competence. This information is based on my many years of experience, both personal and professional. In addition, I interviewed a number of successful women about their experiences with confidence. Once you meet them, I'm sure you'll agree that this is a diverse and amazing group. It includes entrepreneurs, senior executives, a senior leader in the Girl Scouts, the first African-American female combat pilot, authors, speakers, and media personalities. These powerhouses help drive home the importance of *The Confidence Effect*. So let's get started.

The Confidence + Competence Toolkit

Throughout her career, Laura has been putting in long hours. She rarely misses a day. She prides herself on her hard work. She's always the first to arrive at the office and the last to leave. And she's a busy mother in addition to holding her full-time job. During meetings, she usually has ideas and valuable insights to contribute to the conversation, but she doesn't speak up unless she's positive her solution or response is pitch perfect. There are some new leadership opportunities in her company, and Laura wants to move up.

What Laura doesn't know, however, is that she's unlikely to get a promotion. Why? Like many women, Laura thinks working hard and doing a good job is enough to get her promoted. Yet she lacks confidence and a strong professional "brand." She hasn't yet learned to ask for what she deserves. Laura hasn't built a strong network of allies and champions, and sadly she doesn't even know what information she's missing, because she also lacks awareness of her own style—and how to go about changing it for optimized career success.

But there is hope. Laura already has the solutions to her own problems. She needs to build a "confidence + competence toolkit" to help move her out of the role she is in. Part of her problem is that she is not connected to people who can inform her about opportunities. Consequently, other people get picked for roles for which she would have been perfect, but she never knew that the opportunities existed. Laura is one of her company's biggest assets—and her own worst enemy.

As you can imagine, Laura isn't alone. Many female employees face silent, challenging realities on a daily basis. This is inspiring some of the nation's strongest and most celebrated female business leaders to speak out about the future of women in corporate America.

When it comes to women in business, Laura is in the majority, i.e., not in a leadership position. In fact, according to *Forbes* magazine, while women make up almost half, or 46.9 percent, of the modern workforce, "40 percent of large companies have no women on their boards and only 5 percent of startups are owned by women."

And, according to "Unlocking the Full Potential of Women at Work," a special report by McKinsey & Company, "Leaders make gender diversity a priority because they see the prize: a talent advantage that's hard to replicate. But few companies are winning that prize. The top circles of leadership remain male bastions; women make up just 14 percent of Fortune 500 executive committees, and there are few women CEOs. Although corporate leaders are working hard to change this, progress remains elusive."

With so few women in positions of leadership, those who are feel a responsibility to speak out on behalf of the marked disparity between female and male leaders in the workforce.

According to Arianna Huffington, Founder of *The Huffington Post*, "Women still have an uneasy relationship with power and the traits necessary to be a leader. There is the internalized fear that if we are really powerful, we are going to be considered ruthless or pushy or strident—all those epithets that strike at our femininity. We are still working at trying to overcome the fear that power and womanliness are mutually exclusive."

This could explain why in 2014, 95 percent of all venture capital went to men; of the top 2,500 corporate executives in America, only 63 were women; only three Fortune 500 companies were headed by women; and Congress was 90 percent male!

Sheryl Sandberg, COO of Facebook, former VP of online sales and operations for Google, and author of the bestselling book *Lean In: Women, Work, and the Will to Lead*, says, "We need women at all levels, including the top, to change the dynamic, reshape the conversation, to make sure women's voices are heard and heeded, not overlooked and ignored."

Sandberg's words are particularly resonant in the technology industry from which she hails, where only 25 percent of the workforce and less than 5 percent of startup owners are women. Recently, Microsoft CEO Satya Nadella made front-page news around the world when he suggested women should not ask for raises but simply rely on "karma" to take care of them. Nadella's comments highlighted the pervasive and unconscious bias that affects so many women in the workplace today.

And finally, in a fiery call to arms, Rachel Sklar—blogger and Founder of Change the Ratio, a group that seeks to increase visibility and opportunity for women in technology and new media—sums up the way many women in business feel: "There's a benefit to including women, there's a benefit to considering women, there's a benefit to writing about women, and there's a benefit to having women included in everything. And I think it's ridiculous that this is a situation I have to be defensive about."

Clearly, I couldn't agree more!

The Confidence Effect

With nearly 35 years of corporate and executive coaching experience, and as an author, consultant, trainer, speaker, and CEO, I have seen too many similar stories and felt the pain of rejection alongside my clients. Many of them, like Laura, come to me confused and feeling as if they are missing something, and they leave feeling clued in, competent and, above all, confident.

At the Half The Sky Leadership Institute, my program for women who want to strengthen their leadership skills, business acumen, and executive presence, I work with many women like Laura. I have learned a great deal through these experiences, and this book allows me the opportunity to share the skills women need to navigate the political culture in the workplace in order to receive that next promotion—and so much more.

Every woman is the CEO of her own career and life. Through one-on-one executive coaching, group workshops, and keynote presentations, I have helped thousands of women advance their leadership skills, develop their personal brands, and reach for the next level in their careers.

My goal is to inspire people to move beyond barriers to achieve sustainable success, both professionally and in their personal lives. My company provides executive coaching, leadership development, and consulting in the Birkman Method,® a powerful assessment tool that identifies a client's interests, behaviors, underlying motivations, and needs.

The Confidence Effect: Every Woman's Guide to the Attitude That Attracts Success is about showing women how to connect their competence to their confidence. My goal is to help you speak out, take risks, and assume leadership positions with assurance. There is plenty of research to pinpoint why and how women are in their current position. I want to help them move beyond the data to what's really important: how to become more confident, one step at a time.

Let's take these next steps together.

Moving from Competence to Confidence

We just decided to go out there and be aggressive and be strong and courageous and not be afraid.

—Gabby Douglas, American
Olympic gymnast

In order to be truly confident, it's critical to understand the delicate relationship between competence and confidence as they apply to our workplace brand as well as our leadership potential. Both are equally important, but for too long it seems women have relied on competence rather than confidence to show off their skills.

As a result, we find ourselves at a point in time when there are more women in the workforce than ever, yet we remain woefully underrepresented in leadership positions at the top, or even the near top.

According to the Center for American Progress, "Women . . . hold almost 52 percent of all professional-level jobs . . . and since 2002, have outnumbered men in earning undergraduate business degrees. And yet, women have not moved up to positions of prominence and power in America at anywhere near the rate that they should have based on their representation and early successes in higher education and in the entry-level workforce."

There are so many reasons why this observation is so dreadfully accurate that it would take reams of paper to list them all. That's not my intention. This book isn't about men in the workplace. Men are not the enemy. This is about connecting with our own power as leaders and taking ownership of the areas in which we can effect change.

This book is about what you can do right now, today, to turn the tide in your life. For most of my 30 years in corporate America, I lived the workplace reality described in the Center for American Progress quote. This book is about how I beat the odds by overcoming the obstacles, detours, and roadblocks in my path to success.

What I've discovered along my own personal journey to authenticity, leadership, and career satisfaction is that competence is absolutely critical to success. You must be good at what you do. You must exceed expectations. But competence is only half the equation. You need to combine it with *confidence* to truly crack the code.

Growth Comes from Within: Tapping into Your Core of Confidence

Writing for *The Atlantic* magazine, Katty Kay and Claire Shipman, authors of the book *The Confidence Code: The Science and Art of Self-Assurance—What Women Should Know* (Harper-Business, 2014), provide a great definition of confidence. "Confidence is not, as we once believed, just feeling good about yourself," they write. "If women simply needed a few words of reassurance, they'd have commandeered the corner office long ago. Perhaps the clearest, and most useful, definition of confidence we came across was the one supplied by Richard Petty, a psychology professor at Ohio State University, who has spent decades focused on the subject. 'Confidence,' he told us, 'is the stuff that turns thoughts into action.' "

Renowned executive and life coach Gail Blanke defines confidence as "An attitude that starts with the conviction that you're here for a reason and that you are so much more powerful, so much better, so much more necessary to the world than you have any idea."

Jennifer Dieas, the Founder and CEO of tanning services Golden Girl Chicago and Glowout Salon, defines confidence as ". . . the ability to go from trial to trial without letting it break your spirit. There are daily turbulent situations that we could go through, but if you're confident and you believe in your vision and what you're doing and your purpose, then it never rattles you too much, because you always can come back to that center of knowing what you're doing and what your purpose is."

So, what does it mean to possess *The Confidence Effect*? It means confidence to the *core*—the place where we're the most powerful, the most authentic, the most self-reliant, and the most connected to our skills and abilities. If you hang out in a gym or talk to a personal trainer or just keep up with fitness magazines or websites, you hear a lot about building your core because that's where you're flexible and have the most strength.

I like the idea of the core as it relates to confidence for women, in particular, because that is where we house our strength and power—where we find our voice. And by strengthening our confidence and connecting it to our competence, we can become more powerful in our organizations and in our lives. It is from our cores that we move forward into the types of leadership positions that now exist mostly in our dreams.

I developed *The Confidence Effect* gradually over more than 30 years of experience working with women. I facilitated executive leadership programs for 13 years, was an executive in the talent space, and now I operate a unique leadership institute that helps high-potential women become high-impact leaders.

Experts in the field such as McKinsey and the *Harvard Business Review* have compiled a ton of research that I could quote extensively. But instead of dispensing facts, I want to have a conversation about the many women I see who simply are not moving beyond a certain level in their organizations.

They are, in a word, stuck. They've been working deep in the trenches, outperformed their contemporaries, led teams or maybe even divisions, but the corner office or even senior management seems to elude them. Why? What's holding them back?

Gravitas: Grit at the Center of Confidence

When you talk to women about those questions, their answers are rarely about performance. Instead, they usually talk about confidence—and specifically about women's hesitancy to take risks, speak up, stand out, or even raise our hands. We question our own competence, feel like we're under a microscope, and perhaps even feel unable to meet the demands of leadership positions. As a result, we miss out on building the relationships and workplace brand that can put us where we want to go and give us the confidence we need to take risks, believe in ourselves, and perform to our potential.

An extension of our core confidence is the power we bring—or don't bring—to our workplace roles. *Gravitas* is the presence we feel deep down inside. *Merriam-Webster* defines it as "high seriousness (as in a person's bearing or in the treatment of a subject)." Without this air of gravitas—the sense of weight and "grit" deep in our guts—it's hard to feel the confidence we need to lead: to lead ourselves, our teams, our divisions, and, ultimately, our organizations.

Citing gravitas as a key ingredient of executive presence, the Center for Talent Integration describes it as encompassing confidence, poise under pressure, and decisiveness. Gravitas lends an air of credibility—of *gravity*—to our actions. It adds weight, depth, and character to our personalities, and it allows us to temper our emotions with data, analysis, and proven, delivered results. I call this grit. It's the ability to stand your ground and express your strength in an appropriate, professional manner.

I often use the wonderful expression "No grit, no pearl" to remind my clients of their need to "stand over their own power"—not to waiver, but to own the moment, to feel the grit, and to stand strong. Gail Blanke agrees. "The importance of grit—or resilience—is that most of us don't know how good we are until we get to the hard part and the power of persistence and simply keeping going and refusing to cave, which is always very tempting," she says.

Lily Kelly-Radford, Ph.D., President of LEAP Leadership, Inc., an executive coaching firm, explains, "Gravitas lets you know that you're in the company of a real leader. . . . [I]t is showing grace under pressure. It involves intellectual horsepower, but it also decisiveness—and showing teeth. In other words, demonstrating that you can stand alone on an issue whether people agree with you or not, but not as a hostile person; it's not always feeling like you have to fold."

So if women are not showing up confidently, proudly, and ready and willing to lead, if we're not raising our hands or stepping forward with that grit and power behind us, then, typically, the organization overlooks us and promotes men. Why? Because men tend to exhibit those traits even if they're not as competent. They show up, stand out, raise their hands, take charge—even take command—regardless of whether they possess the skills such leadership positions demand.

If we strengthen our cores, if we focus on getting to the heart of the matter and positioning ourselves in a way that is both competent and confident, then we have the power within us to show up, stand out, and lead in a way that's authentic to our true and inner strengths. We don't have to wait until we are fully confident to begin to exhibit confident behaviors. We can, in fact, "act as if" and "fake it till we make it." Ines Temple, President and CEO of Lee Hecht Harrison, Peru, shares, "I learned some mantras years ago that I repeat to myself when I'm in certain situations. They are 'I'm strong, I'm able, and I'm calm.' After repeating them to myself several times, I start feeling better and believing in myself again. The other one is 'I'm disciplined, I'm energized, and I'm inspired.' These all do wonders for my self-esteem."

Success is about striking the right balance between competence and confidence. And let me say right off the bat: Confidence alone won't cut it. Bravado, bluster, and popularity alone
won't get you where you want to go. We've all known supremely
confident men and women who, despite their gravitas, simply
don't execute. They don't deliver, they don't delegate, and they
don't meet deadlines. They use emotions rather than facts and
logic. As a result, they are incompetent.

We must be careful not to assume that success is merely a
case of "inserting confidence" and solving all of our workplace
troubles. Just like at the gym, if you work only on your core
and you don't build up your cardio strength, then you won't be
fit overall. Similarly, if you're confident but you lack important
qualities such as business acumen and the knowledge of how to
build relationships, you do not have what it takes to lead.

Showing Up, Standing Out, and
Taking Charge: The 4 Rs of Success

This book will systematically teach you—or perhaps remind
you—how to gain confidence so that it enhances and accelerates
the competence you already possess. The path we'll take is what
I call my *4 Rs of Success*:

o *Relationships*. We can't go it alone, nor should we try.
  Relationships are at the center of *The Confidence Effect*
  because they allow us to network in a way that accelerates both our personal and career growth.

o *Reputation*. How you perceive yourself has a huge influence on how others perceive you. Reputations, like
  respect, are earned. This book will show you how to let

what's inside out so that you can show more of your true, authentic self at work—and everyplace else.

○ *Results*. If we are to believe in ourselves and allow others to believe in us, we must deliver results. Confidence is like a mirror we hold up to reflect our accomplishments; the more we deliver, the more confidence we have.

○ *Resilience*. Finally, we must have the big picture in mind to weather the storms, rise to the challenges, and avoid the potholes and outright roadblocks that are part and parcel of our ultimate journey to success. According to Sophia A. Nelson, author of *The Woman Code: 20 Powerful Keys to Unlock Your Life* (Revell, 2014), "Being resilient is really what life's all about. It really comes down to that. Life is going to knock you down. Life is going to challenge you, it's going to test you, it's going to push you, it's going to pull you, it's going to do a lot to you . . . and you've got to be ready for that." All of us will stumble and fail over our lifetimes and careers. Resilience is the ability to bounce back.

At the heart of each R you will find confidence. That's because it's important for women not only to step up and say "I've got this," but also to really believe it.

Profile in Confidence:
Dawn Callahan, Chief Marketing Officer, Boingo Wireless

I had an experience with an event I was attending. Everyone was scheduled to meet in the hotel for a mixer before a weeklong leadership program I was attending.

It was a casual affair and I remember sitting in my hotel room, about 20 minutes away from having to go down and meet everybody. I was absolutely terrified that I had to go meet all of these people because I felt like I was—not worthy. I shouldn't have been included in the program. I was way too junior compared to all of these fancy people with these fancy titles who were also going to be fellows that year with me.

And I fell into this kind of imposter syndrome, like, "They are going to find out that I'm nothing special" and it's going to be awful. I remember calling a friend and saying, "Oh my God." She talked me down. I went down there and met 25 people who could not have been nicer. We did this introductory exercise where we were asked our feelings about being there.

And it was interesting that almost every woman in the room—and these people are presidents, chief officers, executive vice presidents, SVPs of their companies, very, very accomplished women—almost every single one said exactly what I was feeling 20 minutes prior, which was that they were terrified to come in and meet the rest of these women . . . they were all terrified that they wouldn't measure up, either.

And I was like, "I deserve this, right? I am only a director, I'm the junior man on the totem pole here, but this lady sitting right next to me is the chief marketing officer of a major network. How can she not feel confident? Right? How does that happen?"

What I realized—and it was probably one of the most important lessons that I ever realized in my life—is that everybody feels terrified when they have to walk into a room like this situation. And when you realize that "Oh my God, everybody is in the exact same scenario," it really takes the power out of it.

So, my key learning that I would share with other people is: "Guess what? Every single person—no matter what her title is or how much she's accomplished—goes through life a little bit terrified, and you just sort of fake it till you make it because your insides do not have to match your outsides and that's okay. Just know that you can show up and appear to be confident, even if you're not. Because everybody else is in that exact same scenario, too." So it sort of normalizes the situation.

I think people can build up their confidence by understanding that there is no such thing as someone who has got it all together. The trouble comes when we constantly compare ourselves to other people, or to our perceptions of other people. So, when you take that away—this falsehood that this person over here, we'll call her Jane, has it all together and she performs better than me—and you start to realize that, hey, Jane is also terrified, that Jane struggles with x, y, or z . . .

You start to realize, okay, there's nothing I have to be afraid of. So, I think that one of the things that you have to do is get in control of the voice that's in your head. That's easier said than done. Here I am sharing all of this like pearls of wisdom, like I have achieved this and I know how to do this.

That is an absolute falsehood. I have no clue how to tame the voices in my head because they are strong and negative and very good at making me feel small. So I try to master the self-talk with that confidence exercise.

Take It from Me: Confidence Counts

This book isn't based entirely on science. Nor is it based exclusively on the status of the women I coach, counsel, speak to, and engage with.

Some comes from personal experience. Case in point: the numerous promotions I did not get. In hindsight, I recognize that it was less about not getting promoted than it was about not raising my hand and promoting myself for the position. Until I was in my 30s I lived in that "good girl" space. You know the one I'm talking about. If I work hard and keep my head down—and say "yes" to everything, and put my family, my health, my very life on hold—then I will ultimately get noticed, get promoted, and it will have been worth it.

Working for a large national retailer, I missed out on opportunities because I was unable, or unwilling, to recognize my own worth. There I was, managing human resources for 4,000 employees and making $58,000 a year, and not once in 13 years did I ask for a raise, promotion, or title improvement. I just thought that as long as I was "good," I would get rewarded. But the truth was, not only did I *not* get rewarded but I wasn't even *regarded*! And when I did finally ask to be promoted from manager to director, I was told "no" without an explanation or opportunity to discuss the reasons.

Looking back, this moment was a turning point. I was in shock that the company I had believed in didn't believe in me, and I realized something about myself that day: I had neither the confidence nor the skills to ask for what I wanted and to position it professionally, not emotionally. According to Sophia A. Nelson, "I think the biggest factor in determining whether or not a woman is confident and able to successfully pursue her desires and dreams is if she knows her value. And if she doesn't know her value as a woman or as a person, she'll never have confidence."

I believe that as women, we expect to be treated fairly. When that doesn't happen, we grow frustrated, and sometimes we leave. That's exactly what I did. I quit the company I was with for 13 years because I felt disillusioned, disappointed, and, frankly, disrespected.

When I look back, though I'm glad I left the organization, I realize I mismanaged the situation in part by letting it go on for too long. Who knows what my future there might have held if only I'd had the confidence to treat myself as well as I expected the company to treat me.

But regret and resentment are a waste of time. It's like trying to drive a car when you're looking only in the rearview mirror. The experience turned out to be an opportunity and a lesson.

Later on in my career, I learned how to ask for things. Once, after I had been given a significantly bigger role in an organization, with one day's notice and no additional money or title change, I told my boss that if the company wanted me to continue to work in that capacity, senior management had to make a decision: I deserved to have my compensation and a title commensurate with the added responsibility. Rather than get emotional about it like I had earlier in my career, I built and presented a business case for the promotion—and I was, in fact, promoted.

Even then, the role wasn't necessarily "given" to me. It was not a slam dunk. I had to quantify where I was able to improve the business. I had to make a business case to show that I deserved the promotion. The lead was, "Here are the ways in which I am impacting the business . . . "

Keep in mind that I couldn't have walked into that corner office and asked for that title change and promotion if I hadn't already delivered; that was the key to my competence and my confidence.

You have to be able to back up what you're saying. It's not just about being confident, and it's never about being overconfident. Lisa Chang, senior vice president of human resources for the AMB Group, explains, "Sometimes when I am interviewing young professionals coming into the workplace, I appreciate the kind of vigor with which they approach things, but it's clear that they're overconfident, that they don't have the credentials to back it up, and I would prefer that they would just be eager but sort of admit to the things that they hadn't done yet. Because if you are on the other side of the table and you have 20 or 30 years' worth of experience and you are looking at what this new person may or may not have done, the way they speak and the confidence that they project, it is that borderline between confidence and arrogance."

Everything I teach—and everything in this book—is designed around *actually delivering results*. You can only go so far on your relationships and your reputation. You've got to cross the finish line. At some point, you have to show up as a leader even if you don't have the title. All of those things show up as the dynamics that affect your own personal leadership brand. You must combine your competence with your confidence.

The Fine Art of Bragging

How do you self-promote in a healthy way? How do you brag without appearing cocky? Or is it okay for women to be cocky? I believe that if we can deliver, we shouldn't minimize our gifts and talents. As Muhammad Ali once said, "It ain't bragging if you can back it up."

If you're positive about your own skill set, folks tend to believe you; they'll want to work with you, for you, or on your behalf. Conversely, if you're working with someone who is critical of her own skills, you start to believe her. There is research that supports the concept of positive disclosure. People like to work with others who are comfortable saying they are good at something.

But there's a fine line between positive disclosure and boasting. I believe that too often, as women, we err on the side of caution and shy away from being what we think is "prideful." Perhaps we do this because we fear it can make us targets to shoot down. Or maybe we don't believe we can back up our own self-praise. The good news is that you don't need to put up your own billboard to self-promote. If you are able to talk confidently about your skill set—and of course back it up with results—it can actually be seen as a positive. The trick is finding that healthy balance between confidence and overconfidence, between making promises and delivering results. Too often we minimize what we do when what we do is actually pretty darn special!

For example, let's say you are the top fundraiser for an organization and someone says, "Congrats, you are our Number 1 fundraiser!" Our first instinct may be to immediately wave it off: "Oh, no, I just got lucky."

Quite often, rather than owning our participation in successful events, we attribute our accomplishments to luck. Even when complimented, we have the tendency to be uncomfortable taking praise. We need to learn how to take compliments, to just own it and say "thank you" and be proud of the things we've done. Because when we deflect a compliment, people are watching. They may believe that we're not good enough, that we didn't deserve it, we didn't earn it, and it was easier than it looked.

Accepting compliments makes them real, not just to us but to others as well. I spoke to a woman recently who'd received industry recognition. When I said I was proud of her and congratulated her on her accomplishment, she said, "They must have run out of people to nominate." That's like taking your power, throwing it on the ground, and stomping on it. Even if she thought the attention was embarrassing, a simple "thank you" would have sufficed.

The key to unlocking confidence lies within. When it comes to self-promotion, we are our own worst enemies. Throughout this book I will share special tools, tips, and strategies for how to comfortably build that confidence from within so that it radiates outward.

Profile in Confidence:
Gail Blanke, President and CEO, Lifedesigns

Confidence is knowing you are able to make exactly the right contributions today without waiting. Most of us sell ourselves short. When you run into really truly confident people, you feel it because they make it about you, not them.

So they're not thinking, "How am I doing? Do they like me? Have I messed up so far?" They're thinking, "How are you? What can I provide that you need?" It's all about listening to the other person rather than always speaking about yourself and trying to prove how good you are. Confident people don't need to prove how good they are. And so I think it's an attitude that propels you outward rather than inward. Remember that wonderful film *A League of Their Own*, about the women's professional baseball teams that played during the 1940s?

Geena Davis was the catcher. Tom Hanks was the manager of the team. Geena comes up to Tom Hanks and says, "Okay, that's it. I quit." And he said, "Quit? Why in the world would you quit?" And she said, "It just got too hard." And he says, "Hard? It's supposed to be hard. If it wasn't hard, everybody would do it." And then he says this great line: "It's the hard that makes it great."

So, it's supposed to be hard. Otherwise, somebody would have already done it.

The Takeaway

Allow me to make one more case for confidence, and it's a biggie: For me, confidence is the ultimate game changer. I would love you to take a mental snapshot of yourself right now, while you are at the beginning of this book, and then again once you've reached the end. My hope for you—and my goal in writing this book—is that you walk away with the tools and insights you need to become more confident than you were when you began. Simple changes, applied over time, can make a significant shift not only in how others see you but how you see yourself.

Let us officially recognize, here and now, that your confidence and your competence are equally important—that your ability to do the work is valuable—but as you try to grow and learn as a leader, it may become an issue if you can't lift yourself up and ask for what you want.

Being competent without being confident is like working alone in the dark. You may be able to get your work done, but who would know about it? Confidence allows you to shine a light on your ability—without bragging or "billboarding." It's about turning the light on so people can see what you are doing—and ultimately provide you with the opportunities you seek.

At the end of the day, we are the CEO of our own lives. We spend too much time worrying about being a beacon for others as opposed to finding out what we are doing to illuminate and create our own power. Your power will lift others, for sure, but you've got to believe that you are more than the sum of your parts. You must be able to say, "I've got this!"

Confidence isn't static. It means constantly auditing yourself and putting a light on your best skills. Confidence is attractive. It multiplies and invites others to share in your success. And that's what makes it a game changer!

So as the CEO of your own life and career, if you are ready to change your game, embrace new challenges, reach new heights, and embrace the leader you were born to be, I invite you to turn the page and begin your journey to greater confidence and, ultimately, to success and happiness.

PART ONE

Relationships

I've always believed that one woman's success can only help another woman's success.
—Gloria Vanderbilt, artist, author,
actress, heiress, and socialite

The first tool in moving from competence to confidence involves understanding and mastering the power of relationships. While many of us feel we should navigate these waters alone, the fact is that powerful relationships can greatly enhance and accelerate our ladder to success.

The Power of Relationships

Our relationships are connected to our networking abilities, which I consider one of the "secret ingredients" to becoming confident to the core. With a strong network in place, full of targeted people and special allies, you can exponentially increase the knowledge base, skill set, and opportunities necessary to enhance, further, and strengthen your career. Relationships are vital to gathering the information we'll need to succeed, as well as developing our in-house brand in the most flattering light.

Many women form fun, lasting, and friendly relationships at work that don't necessarily contribute to their growth as potential leaders but do promote their physical and emotional well-being. This is healthy and good. It enhances our experience at work.

However, the relationships I'm referring to are not only mutually beneficial but powerfully growth-inducing. These "power relationships" are designed to accelerate your career.

Such power relationships come in many different forms:

o The team member who supports, challenges, nurtures, and enlightens you

o The manager who drives you to excel

o The peer who supports, encourages, and aids your desire for personal and professional growth

o The mentor who continually questions and challenges your choices, often with a positive result

o The people you trust who tell you the truth

o The leader who inspires you

o The powerful allies and sponsors who can open doors and provide you with opportunities

It's important to remember that valuable relationships are not static but are always shifting, evolving, growing, and changing. Peers become managers, managers become leaders, and team members get promoted, shifted, downsized, or move on to a different organization. Branches grow and divide. The larger and more powerful your network, the more dynamic, changing, and powerful you become as you grow along with it.

So, factoring all of that in, how you show up for your relationships and whether or not you're considered reliable, innovative, and a team player are all vitally important to your future.

Never forget that as part of an organization, nothing you do exists in a vacuum. Everything you do is either affected by or affects others.

Putting the "Power" in Power Relationships

Unfortunately, many people simply don't realize the value in relationships. As a result, they ignore opportunities to form relationships in favor of "just doing the work." The problem for most people, I think, is that relationships are never black and white, and they have a long shelf life.

Relationships are one of those invisible components that help determine our success. But unlike a pay grade, security clearance, parking space, or job title, you can't necessarily put a finger on how valuable they are . . . until you need them or they need you.

And relationships are always valuable. I can't tell you how many times I've used my network to complete an assignment, fill a position, gather crucial information, host a seminar, write the blurb for a book, answer a question, make an introduction, or somehow improve my life and career.

I'm regularly asked to contribute, aid, assist, mentor, coach, or otherwise influence any number of the people in the key relationships in my professional network—and I do so gladly because over time I have learned that the secret to good relationships is to give as much as you get. Being generous, supportive, and helpful with your network is critical.

Instead, I fear, too many people treat relationships like step-ladders, using them only to get a leg up on the competition, without ever reaching a hand back to help those who are on their way up. These are relationships in name only, the very antithesis of the power relationships that enhance the lives and careers of both parties. One of my favorite expressions is "lift while we climb." We do that by helping others—especially women—as we move up.

Leadership is a cultivated skill and, like any path, follows twists and turns, switchbacks, and pit stops that require us to improvise, adapt, and overcome along the way. We simply can't, and shouldn't, do it alone.

The more relationships you nurture, the more people who are in your network, the more resources you'll have to tap as you successfully navigate your own path to leadership. The fewer relationships you've fostered in and out of the workplace, the fewer resources you'll be able to draw on in times of need.

Sara King, the Principal of Optimum Insights, Inc. and a Faculty Adviser at the Half The Sky Leadership Institute, says, "We cannot underestimate the value of a strong network, which is about developing a variety of relationships, both internal and external. It's really about spending your time building those relationships with people in order to create visibility, in order to have greater understanding of career opportunities and gain more knowledge about your own choices."

Women tend not to spend enough time on networking and building these power relationships, connections, and resources. Then, when they ask for help along their leadership path, they find they are limited in the number of people who can help them succeed. Women are often so busy doing "the work" and taking care of others that they forgo taking care of themselves and building their own networks. We all have time for a coffee or lunch at least once a week with a colleague, mentor, sponsor, ally, or client who can help support our goals as we build our brands.

Mentors, Sponsors, Advocates, and Champions

Many of the women I interviewed for this book were adamant about not just networking effectively but actively seeking out mentors, sponsors, advocates, and champions.

Case in point: EVP and COO of Cox Communications Jill Campbell insists, "I think it's important to listen and get lots of perspectives on yourself. So surround yourself with different people." On the matter of mentors versus sponsors, Jill adds, "People talk a lot about having mentors. I think that's important. But I think it's equally important that you have a sponsor. Women tend to think that their work is going to get them there, but they've got to figure out somebody in the organization who is going to take notice of them and who says, 'Wait a minute! What about Jean? Look at the good work she's doing. I hear she's terrific.' So I think being very deliberate about having a sponsor is important."

Natalye Paquin, Chief Executive Officer of the Girl Scouts of Eastern Pennsylvania, agrees. "Identify advocates and develop an authentic relationship with them," she explains. "I look at advocates as different from coaches or mentors. You know, advocates are at tables that you are not, and they could open doors for you. And they can speak on your behalf, and really fight a battle for you or get in front of you, when you would never have that opportunity or you don't know the opportunities that exist. I think it's really important to develop authentic relationships with individuals who are around tables that are different from yours that you aspire to join so that they can advocate on your behalf."

Vernice "FlyGirl" Armour, whom we met earlier, refers to herself as the CBO, or chief breakthrough officer, for VAI Consulting and Training, LLC. Weighing in on the subject of sponsors, she explains, "Mentors give you guidance and help you out, but sponsors are the people who are willing to bang their fist on the table for you. They speak up at the conference. They're in a position of influence to actually be able to sponsor you into something, which is just essential. Over 74 percent of women are mentored, but they're not promoted that way. Why? Because they don't have the sponsors in place."

Finally, Sara King says, "You have to have people who are advocating for you. There's a lot of language out there—for women—about the differences between mentors and sponsors, and I do think having advocates who are putting your name forward in places that you are not present can't be underestimated."

Relationships Strengthen Your Brand

Simply put, relationships strengthen your network and, in turn, your network strengthens your organizational brand. Remember, all of your workplace behavior reflects on your brand. The stronger your brand, the stronger your confidence level—real and perceived.

For me, the biggest issue surrounding relationships is building your network to ultimately grow your personal brand. I like to say that there is a difference between a network and a support group. A network is an exchange of information, power, and opportunity. A support group is a circle of friends who may support you but not necessarily foster your growth as a potential leader.

Networks and support groups are equally important, but in distinct ways. As I warned earlier, it's important to remember that just having friends and people you enjoy being with is not enough to grow either your network or your personal brand.

The true value of relationships lies in having access to power, resources, and opportunity in ways that wouldn't exist without a network, or even in a limited one with few connections. Just as important, relationships are directly related to your personal brand and how people perceive you as a potential partner, colleague, peer, or leader.

Think of your brand as the unwritten—but undeniable—"echo" that remains after you leave the room. This is a good time to explore your own brand and ask yourself:

o What is left behind for people to remember?

o What is the impression that remains long after you're gone?

o How did you treat people?

o What did you say?

o How did you say it?

o Whom did you say it to?

o How was it received?

All of these issues, and dozens more, contribute to the brand you're creating with each interaction, relationship, and connection. For women in particular, how you treat people and how proficient you are in your current role is what really helps determine how strong—or weak—our personal brands may be. How you interact with people helps determine whether or not they will become allies, sponsors, and mentors.

Profile in Confidence:
Jennifer Dieas, Founder and CEO,
Golden Girl Chicago and Glowout Salon

I feel like confidence is the ability to go from trial to trial without letting it break your spirit. There are daily turbulent situations that we could go through, but if you're confident and you believe in your vision and what you're doing and your purpose, then it never rattles you too much, because you always can come back to that center of knowing what you're doing and knowing what your purpose is. One of the most important things to me is to build solid relationships with other people whom you admire, people who know more than you, so that you can constantly be grooming yourself as you go.

Researching your trade and constantly perfecting and fine-tuning your skill set is super-important. I do that probably six or seven times a year on a major scale where I travel and go to other leaders in my industry, and it's fun to be a client again. So, I think taking yourself out of a leadership role and going back to the basics and being a student is really important.

I moved to Chicago without contacts—without anything. I decided I was going to go full steam and start this business and the concept that I was doing was new, so not only was I a new company but the concept of the service that I was providing was new to people. So I had to be prepared to have a lot of people tell me "no," and to never let that dampen my spirit.

I think that's something that's been able to sustain me, because not everybody is your ideal client, not everybody wants your service or believes in your service, and that's okay. And not everybody believes in how you view your vision and how you view your service, and that's okay, too. There's plenty of abundance . . . plenty of companies and people are free to choose what feels right to them. So I always feel like it's not letting the no's or any kind of outside influence dampen your spirit. You just have to keep going.

Linking In to Stand Out

Another aspect of relationships we'll be covering in this section of the book is how to build them both inside and outside of your current workplace. That's because building relationships in today's world is broader than the people in your office or down the hall from you. A great place to start building relationships outside the workplace is on LinkedIn.com, where your brand is up, running, and on display 24/7/365.

Whether you're looking to expand or simply connect with other professionals in your industry, LinkedIn is a go-to platform where you can highlight your accomplishments, increase your exposure, and stand out. In fact, 70 to 80 percent of job searches actually begin there. LinkedIn is among the first places people go to check out your profile, look at your headshot, and find out about you before you meet. People even use LinkedIn to check out coworkers in their own companies.

Why is exposure outside the office so crucial to potential leaders? In this day and age, social media is not just a powerful tool but a critical skill set to master. When it comes to networking, having a stellar profile on a site like LinkedIn, and knowing how best to navigate its ins and outs, will put you in good standing whether you want to grow in your own organization or get hired by another one.

In essence, LinkedIn is a marketing tool that allows you to control, and even accelerate, how others view your brand. From your profile picture to your description of yourself, to your awards, accomplishments, and education, your brand is accessible to millions of potential network members. Relationships, recommendations, and reputation get impacted—big time—by how you show up on LinkedIn. For better or worse, it can make a real difference in the strength—or weakness—of your brand. Checking up on your LinkedIn network for as few as 10 minutes daily is another way to build relationships that may lead to bigger and better things for you and for those with whom you connect.

One additional aspect to consider: using LinkedIn to make connections in your community. Are you creating the right—or even any—relationships there? Are you exposing yourself to different ways of thinking? Finally, is there an element of diversity to your relationships and how you see the world?

Remember that networks aren't built around the watercooler alone. Branch out—online and into the community—to connect with and build relationships with like-minded, interesting, and encouraging folks.

Relationships take time, care, and nurturing in order to grow, foster, and mature into something mutually beneficial for both parties. Lisa Chang, the SVP of Human Resources whom we met earlier, explains, "If I think about almost every situation where you are trying to build a reputation, or credibility, or a relationship with anyone from a business standpoint, it is always about making that person feel like there is a mutual best interest involved. And if you are overconfident, I think there are times when the other party may feel like, well, that person is not really looking out for my best interest and so that can be a real turnoff. Whereas someone who is truly comfortable and confident can come and talk about how the relationship can be mutually beneficial. It's a series of balancing compromises."

It's hard to create relationships when you're in a crisis. That's why taking the time to attend networking events or to reach out in a positive way to local organizations is an investment in your future that can reap solid benefits when a crisis arises.

The Takeaway

Ultimately, the bonds you build with others, in and around the workplace, strengthen as you continue to foster, take from, and add to the relationship. And, as you can see, building relationships leads to a strong foundation for our next topic: networking.

1

This Is Not Your Mother's Networking

My mom was an Italian citizen who met my dad when he was serving in the U.S. Navy. I was born in Italy, and we moved to the U.S. when I was four years old. By then, my mom was 40 and did not speak or read English. Born in 1923, she'd been taken out of school at the age of eight to help my grandmother take care of her siblings. My mom never had an opportunity to go back to school. Although she was very bright, her circumstances prevented her from having certain educational opportunities. One of the important lessons I learned in my life is that education and intelligence are two different things.

My mom believed that I needed to speak English without an accent and that education was a key to a better life. Since my dad was in the Navy, as soon as we moved to San Diego from Naples, he was back out to sea. He wasn't able to help me learn to read and write in English. Determined to find someone to help me, my mom sought out the only woman in our neighborhood who had a college degree. In 1964, if a woman had a college degree, she was one of three things: a secretary, a teacher, or a nurse. Mary Ryan, a registered nurse, happened to live across the street from us. My mom asked Mary to help me with my homework and my reading/writing skills.

Mary was an Irish fireplug—a little woman with a big personality. She drilled me on my homework and had me read newspapers out loud to practice my speaking skills.

I believe Mary is one of the reasons I did well in school most of my life. She built up my skills, and she told me I was smart and I could do anything I set my mind to. I learned many important lessons from Mary, who was officially my first mentor. But I learned even more important lessons from my mom, who taught me the power of networking. She knew there was something she didn't know, so she found a resource to help me. She walked over to Mary's house with a big bowl of pasta fagioli and said she needed someone to help her little girl learn to read. They forged a friendship (based on Mary's knowledge and my mom's great Italian food).

My mom built her network one woman at a time, and it started with Mary. Over the years, I watched my mom build relationships through community service, being kind and helpful to others, and being willing to ask for (and to give) help. It's a lesson that has served me my entire life.

My mother passed away when I was 24, and Mary Ryan was one of many women who created a safe place for me during that difficult time. Over the course of your life, your network can be activated for lots of different reasons. Mary held the light for me when my mom no longer could. Both of these women helped set my foundation and gave me skills to develop my competence and confidence.

"Shine Your Light" with the Power of Networking

Networking gives us the power to "shine our light" where others can see it, as well as to collaborate with those we can help and—just as important—with those who can help us.

One of the biggest mistakes a future leader can make is thinking that she can lead, or even work, alone. No woman is an island unto herself and, as we've just seen, the larger your network, the more resources you'll have to draw on as you take on more and more leadership roles.

But I don't want to get ahead of myself. Many women think they're networking when, in fact, they're not. So let's begin with a basic definition before we go any further, so that we're both working from the same playbook.

IPO: Information, Power, and Opportunity

For me, networking is quite simply an exchange of three vital components that I like to call IPO:

o *Information.* Networking is first and foremost an information gathering—and giving—exercise. If you're socializing, great, but don't call it networking. Networking can feel like work because it is work, at least when you do it right. If you come away from a social, business, or marketing event and know nothing more than you did when you arrived, then you're not networking. Collecting a handful of business cards is not networking. According to Lisa Chang of AMB Group, "Building a network is surrounding yourself with people who can prop you up when you don't feel like you are in a position to be propped up and having other people to be there to support you. I think that is really important, to surround yourself with people who know your capabilities and, when you start to stumble a little bit, can kind of pick you back up. I think that is really important, to have that network."

○ *Power*. Power comes from knowledge, which is why all three of the IPO components are so vitally important to your networking activities. Don't think of power, in this sense, as a negative, mean, or nasty thing, where you're stepping on others to climb your way up. No, this kind of power comes from the strength of your relationships and how they can help you accelerate and multiply your efforts in times of need. When it comes to leadership, the more people you have in your network, the more powerfully you can lead because you have more resources compared to leaders who isolate themselves from valuable contacts.

○ *Opportunity*. Too many women still think that opportunity will magically waltz into their cubicles and whisk them away to the corner office. They believe that if the world is "fair," they will be promoted. Fact is, opportunity is waiting to be discovered around every corner, in every new relationship, and at every meeting. But first you must approach networking as a treasure hunt instead of a chore. Go about your day welcoming the chance to make new connections or strengthen old bonds and see what opportunities emerge.

We'll cover more on IPO in Chapter 5. For now, remember, when viewed through this lens, you can see how networking can greatly impact your current career trajectory and, what's more, brand you as a determined and connected leader.

New Ways to Network

Once upon a time, networking meant going to a meeting and sitting with your friends. And that's great, that's fun, that's . . . comfortable. But if you're always with the same people, recycling the same old ideas, you're probably socializing, not networking.

Nor does networking mean attending an event and collecting business cards to add to your growing collection, all the while knowing that you'll never actually follow up on contacting any of those people. Today, networking is about going to an event where you are exposed to new ideas—where you meet new people and exchange information.

We should absolutely embrace old friendships and nurture existing contacts, but not to the exclusion of new faces, ideas, and opportunities. Imagine visiting a foreign country and eating only at McDonald's. A burger and fries are fine, but you can get them any time you want back home. How about exploring new cuisine, trying new dishes and flavors, sampling the various tastes that a foreign land offers to those who have never experienced it before?

But that's the problem with never leaving your comfort zone, particularly when it comes to networking: By remaining where things are easy, comfortable, and "safe," you miss out on opportunities that are right around the corner. I'm amazed at the number of women I know who go to events and sit next to someone they already know rather than venture out to meet new people. When they tell me they were at a networking event, I say, "No, you ate dinner with a friend." Going to an event is not networking.

Networking: Not a Speech, But a Conversation

One of the many misconceptions about networking is that it requires a stern, stiff, and well-rehearsed elevator speech with which to introduce (i.e., "sell") yourself and, ostensibly, ask the other person for something: a compliment, an introduction, a business card, a phone number, etc.

But networking is not a speech; it's a free-flowing, ongoing conversation—an exchange of words, ideas, inspirations, support, encouragement, and, above all, opportunities.

But in networking, as in anything else worth doing, you get only as much as you give. And the fact is, the more relationships you have, the more you must give.

That is the lifeblood of networking: the ebb and flow of new people, new connections, new ideas, new ventures, and new opportunities to explore. IPO—information, power, and opportunity—is the fuel that jumpstarts new information and cements new relationships.

One of the most important elements of networking is not just to be "served" but to be of service as well. Finding out how you can help others make connections, providing your contacts with helpful information, and being supportive of your network makes a difference. If all you ever do is take, take, and then take some more, word spreads and that becomes your personal brand. But if you're recognized as someone who is generous with your time and skills, someone who does for others as often as she is done for, then that becomes your much more powerful, and influential, personal brand. And that's the kind of brand that makes networking easier down the line because people will actively seek you out to connect with you and collaborate with you.

That said, don't be shy about helping others—and letting them know how you've helped others! It's important to create a certain level of awareness about yourself when building your brand; doing so will reward you with networking opportunities that you never would have imagined.

Networking in 20 Minutes or Less

Another common misconception about networking is that it's massively time-consuming. Networking *does* take time, especially to do it right, but take heart: You don't have to create a vast and thriving network overnight!

One of the first places to start networking is within your own organization, and it's much easier than you think. In fact, here is my simple, proven method for *Networking in 20 Minutes*:

o Start by identifying a skill set that you are looking to improve upon or even master, such as marketing, promotion, technology, or social media. Let's say you're an expert in marketing but you struggle with budgeting.

o Reach out to someone in the finance division of your company to set up a brief, 20-minute meeting.

o Offer to buy the finance person a cup of coffee; make it convenient for her and stress that you won't take up a lot of time. Typically, I find, 20 minutes is enough to get to know each other better, connect, and share vital information.

o During this meeting, talk briefly about your diverse skill sets and, most important, *offer something in return*. For example, after learning a bit more about budgeting, perhaps you can make a few marketing suggestions to her, such as how to make a more effective presentation.

I'm a big believer in going outside of your area to continually improve your own skill set and that of others. So if you are in marketing, get to know the operations side of your company a little better; become familiar with the real "guts" of the organization.

Branch out of your comfort zone, broaden your horizons, and introduce yourself to folks you wouldn't seek out if you weren't interested in growing your network.

The Locked Gate: Networking for Mentors

Most people would kill for a little guidance now and then, which is why finding a good mentor is a critical step to success for any future leader. Unfortunately, finding a mentor can be challenging because most people who have the experience, wisdom, skill sets, and leadership to mentor you are so busy being successful that they won't have time to mentor anyone! However, as you network and expand your skills, you will prove yourself to be someone worth mentoring. Consequently, you'll come into contact with more potential mentors.

For example, a young man who was my intern many years ago has always kept in touch with me through updates on what's happening in his career in professional sports. My network is broad, and whenever someone in it needs talent, a connection, or a contact in the sports field, he's on the top of my list. Whether it's to ask for information or offer a position, the relationship is a valuable one because it provides the IPO that makes networking so rich in opportunities.

One great way to have access to prominent thought leaders and potential mentors is to make time to volunteer at various events, seminars, conferences, and speaking engagements. There's a great need for such volunteers to help with registration, direct traffic, escort speakers, and so forth at these events. Being part of the process gives you exposure to a variety of interesting and well-connected people.

Having been a keynote speaker at dozens of events, I can tell you that the volunteers are the ones I tend to speak with the most, especially as I'm going through my microphone check sessions and preparing to speak. You'd be surprised by how quickly you can create an impression just by making a guest speaker's life a little easier!

Networking: The Social Media Shift

Networking has evolved since the advent of social media, but despite the rapid advancement of technology, I think that at its heart, networking is still basically the same. I do, however, have more access to people than I used to. And, thanks to email and texting and social media sites like LinkedIn, I have the ability to communicate quickly with my network in ways that didn't exist five years ago.

But while the access and speed with which you can connect with people is different today, what people want and expect is the same. People want you to be authentic and not to contact them just because you want something. Using your network only when you are in need or in a crisis is a mistake.

People I haven't heard from in years will call me, panicking and looking for help when they lose jobs or go through a restructuring of their organization. I do my best. Yet, I can't help but wonder when, and if, they'll ever return the favor.

On the other hand, I have folks in my network who are in essence partners from whom I don't wait for a call before I send information, power, or opportunity (IPO) their way. You have to express gratitude along the way and stay in touch with the people in your network. Otherwise, frankly, they're not part of your network. Someone you haven't spoken to in 10 years may still be in your network, but in name only.

Another way that networking has changed is the "stickiness" that accompanies your personal brand as it merges and evolves into your online brand. In essence, your network and brand get interconnected.

Here's an example: I know of someone who had a strong professional brand but began making provocative social media posts. People's perception of this individual began to shift, and members of her network began to disengage from her. When you go off track in terms of appropriateness, it can really change people's perception of you.

The speed at which people can actually begin to disengage from you has also sped up. We have to be careful not only in how we network but how we communicate within our organizations and also within our larger network online.

The Takeaway

It's a mistake to think that you can do it all alone. The more resources you have to draw on, the more you can accomplish. Keep in mind that while socializing is fine, it's not networking. Nor is networking merely attending an event and collecting business cards if you have no plan to follow up. Networking is about getting exposed to new ideas, meeting new people—including potential mentors and partners—and exchanging information. Think of it as an exchange of three vital components that make up IPO: information, power, and opportunity.

2

Delegation: Working Harder Isn't the Answer

For too many women, working hard seems to be the answer to everything, as if by doing everything, all at once, by ourselves, we can prove we're worthy of that promotion, raise, or corner office. But in doing so, we may overlook those team and subordinate relationships that can help us achieve more, with less.

This chapter on delegation skills focuses on one of the most overlooked and underrated workplace relationships around. Learning to delegate allows you the space and time to lift your head among the crush of work and build your brand and network. The energy we use doing everything ourselves can keep us feeling (and looking) overwhelmed and harried at work. Delegation is another tool to help you connect your competence to your confidence. Looking like your hair is on fire does not instill confidence in your skills.

Don't Micromanage

Like many corporate buzzwords, *delegation* carries with it a lot of baggage. As we assume more, and greater, responsibilities in our ascension through the ranks of leadership, naturally we can't keep doing the things we did two or even three positions ago.

We have new responsibilities, yet we cling to our old work ethic of doing it twice as long, and twice as hard, as everyone else. Some of us may see delegation as a crutch, something the guys use to get things done while they're out golfing. But like networking, delegation is a secret weapon savvy leaders use to accelerate both their personal brand and daily performance.

When it comes to delegation, we often get in our own way. I have seen many women get so torn up over the "housekeeping" issues of how to delegate—the nuts and bolts and ins and outs—that they decide it's not worth the effort. I think women are consumed with "how to do it" and "what the value is."

As we get into more senior roles, our work should become less tactical (operational) and more strategic (high-level leadership). Yet, the women we work with at the Half The Sky Leadership Institute are often extremely protective of "their" way of doing things. Essentially, they're saying, *"We've been rewarded for doing our work a certain way. If we give that up, we'll lose ground."*

They get protective of the work that has gotten them into a higher position, and they tend to feel that if their name is attached to something, their handiwork should be all over it. They're coveting their own personal brand. Perhaps they've found that past partners have either let them down or not shown the same work ethic. As a result, they don't delegate. They try to keep all that work under their brand. They do it all themselves.

Sara King suggests that women refrain from what she calls "volunteering for work." According to her, "All that does is increase your workload and doesn't increase your value. It's not uncommon that women fall into the trap of wanting to be seen as a go-to person or wanting to feel that they measure up or have done enough or are good enough, so we tend to volunteer trying to demonstrate our worth, and instead, all we end up doing is adding to our workload."

Another problem with trying to do it all yourself is that you're not where you were two or three positions ago, when the tactical was more immediate than the strategic. Leadership didn't promote you to do what you've always done, but to do what it needs done, often at a much higher level. Your company's leaders need your full attention on the tasks at hand, and quite frankly, they *expect* you to delegate those things you don't need to do yourself.

That's why, just like having a powerful network, having a team of "power players" is critical to helping you keep an eye on the strategic while letting others help you with the tactical. Trying to do it all yourself, no matter how capable you are, is doomed to fail. Trying to do too many things at once creates more room for error.

Jill Campbell of Cox Communications says, "I always tell people to accentuate their positives. Not everybody is good at everything. So particularly when you get into leadership positions, surround yourself with people who have the skill sets that you are weaker on. I'm a firm believer in hiring really excellent people because then you look good and you have less to do. So you promote them, you get them what they need, and it works both ways. Try to find people who could replace you if you got hit by a car tomorrow. And so that builds confidence in them as well because you're allowing them to grow."

Even for women leaders who do delegate, there's a challenge: I've seen plenty of women managers who delegate work to someone else, and then, in an effort to ensure that the work lives up to the organization's brand, they end up micromanaging how everything gets done along the way. Not only does this mean that you're working as hard as if you did the work yourself, but it also limits your team's creativity, confidence, and growth. You can't elevate yourself or your team if you're always looking over their shoulders and guiding them on every little thing; that's not delegation by any stretch of the imagination.

True delegation relies on trust: trusting team members to do the job to your standards even when you're not there to micromanage them every step of the way. I know it can be a challenge. We may have had bad experiences with delegation in the past, handing off critical assignments to less than stellar performers, only to wind up with egg on our faces. Don't let one apple spoil the whole bunch. That's why I included the topic of delegation in this section about relationships. When it comes to delegation, it's all about finding the right people to partner with on your way to the top.

The Dangers of Not Delegating

Women laugh when I tell them there are dangers of not delegating, until I warn them that it could seriously impact their chances of promotion. How could that be? Well, it starts at the entry level when, like most women, you are dead set on proving yourself by doing twice as much as any of the other new hires, twice as hard, and twice as fast.

Trust me. I've been there. Accommodating to a fault, we are happy to take on as many duties, as often as needed, to the point where we build a reputation as the go-to gal for any and all tasks everybody else is eager to delegate. We do them so well and so graciously that we become too valuable where we are—and end up missing key opportunities—all because we put ourselves last.

It's frustrating, unfair, and, unfortunately, far too common in the modern workplace. Part of it is that company leaders know it would probably take two or three new hires to replace you. But there's something else: They may also fear that you won't delegate once you're a leader because you can't delegate in your current position.

They know you do it all yourself—the office "steady Eddie"—and, as a result, you simply don't get promoted. Bottom line: If we don't make delegation a critical leadership competency, it falls by the wayside for some of us and, consequently, we have no ability to delegate.

Profile in Confidence:
Andrea Agnew, Executive Director of Workforce Diversity and Inclusion, Comcast Cable

I'll start with what confidence looks like to me. It is the ability to confront any given issue and respond in a way as if it was solving a problem. I think that confidence manifests itself in women in very different ways. So whether it's around family, relationships, or work, I think women have a way of dissecting the problem and trying to get to a solution. I think that's how it manifests in women.

There are five key things I think you should focus on when working on your confidence. I think the first one is to know what you really want to do and where you really want to go. I have conversations with people day in and day out talking about how they're ready for the next role, they're ready to make a move, but they're not sure about what that move is. So the first thing is to know where you want to go, and be definite about that. What you want to do and where you want to go.

The second thing I would say is to make sure you have the skill set that gets you there. And if you don't, then begin building that skill set to get you there. You have to take a self-inventory to make sure that you are ready to get there.

The third thing I would say is to hone your business acumen. And I say that because business happens in very different places. It can happen over a happy hour after work. It could happen on the way to go get coffee. It could happen on a golf course. It could happen in any type of setting. So hone your business acumen and your financial business acumen as well.

Fourth, I would say, is work on developing others. I think the greatest asset for leaders is to build their legacy while they're living. And the more that you give a little bit away to someone else, the longer your legacy lives. There is that old adage: Your light doesn't dim because you light someone else's candle. I think there is enough room in the sunshine for us all, but a true leader builds other leaders, they don't build followers.

And the fifth thing is to be hungry for what it is you want. And that could be getting healthy emotionally, physically, mentally, spiritually, or financially. You've got to be hungry for those things and get those things in order as well, because those are key things that not only get you to build your career but help your career to be sustainable. Each of these things helps build and sustain confidence, both personally and professionally.

The Takeaway

Ultimately, delegation needs to become a part of your professional toolkit, not as a once-only "event" but as an institutional habit that helps others identify you as a potential leader who knows the importance of strategy over tactics. Think of it as an arm of your networking efforts, building a strong team of powerful partners you trust, implicitly, to help you achieve twice as much, twice as often—and twice as well!

3

The Keys to Executive Presence

One of the most pivotal workplace relationships is the one we have with ourselves. When we believe we are worthy, then we act as if we are worthy and achieve unbelievable results through what has been called "executive presence," or that air of leadership that pervades our personal brand and follows us wherever we go.

In other words, executive presence is how we show up, the image we present, and how effectively we communicate. Many people talk about executive presence, but they don't all agree on its definition. The Center for Talent Innovation did some groundbreaking research on this topic. The study breaks executive presence into three main components:

o *Gravitas*. This is the unspoken "weight" you carry around with you evoking leadership qualities and inspiring others to follow you. Gravitas is the kind of seriousness that lets others know you mean business and that you expect the same of them.

o *Communication*. How we communicate is not just about the way we speak to others, but what we say. Are we truthful, diplomatic, and thoughtful, or simply tossing off bumper-sticker platitudes we've read on our favorite leadership blog? People like to know you're authentic and true to your word, and nothing conveys it like an open line of communication that gives as good as it gets.

o *Appearance*. This is not just your physical appearance, of course, but also the important, higher-level issue of how you "appear" to others as you circulate around the office. It's how you comport yourself at meetings and the general, overall image you present as you go about your day. Do you wonder about your appearance? If not, you should. And even if you do, you may want to look past your mirror at the way you act as well as how you look.

At the Half The Sky Leadership Institute, we try to help women understand how they "show up" at the workplace—that is, how to craft their own individual executive presence. Make no mistake: This is not about being the best salesperson but about becoming confident in your skills and learning to deliver. It's about showing up as a leader in a way that meets the expectations of others. And a key part of that is being comfortable with this presence and having it work for you.

Ellen East, chief communications officer of Time Warner Cable, explains, "I think confidence boils down to being comfortable in your own skin, and I don't think that manifests itself in women in any one way, and I think that's a wonderful thing. I think a lot of women find confidence in dressing appropriately for the event or the occasion. In kind of making sure they aren't going to stand out. And other women find confidence in making sure that they *do* stand out. They'll wear the brightest dress in the room, or have the crazy hairstyle, or whatever. And I think that's terrific, that women have reached a point that they can express themselves and feel confidence looking the way they want to look."

Executive presence is not about presenting a false front or polishing your facade until it shines, but carefully cultivating your self-image to achieve your full potential. In terms of influencing, this is where you have to flex your muscle, your power, and your understanding of the key strengths you already have— and need to develop.

The Power of Presentations

You can be quite a powerful leader in your own right, but . . . do people know it? Part of executive presence is communicating in such a way that you are heard as well as recognized. Every leader, over time, builds a successful brand—but not by accident.

Various aspects of leadership include the ability to build relationships, garner resources, and complete tasks. But, at least for women, one little known secret about successful leadership is the ability to do things to help people know who you are. Branding is about visibility. It's about making sure that others know what you look like and how you "show up." In other words, your personal brand is how you display your executive presence to individuals as well as to groups.

Speaking—actual speech patterns, tone of voice, and credibility—matter more than you may think. Take it from Natalie Nixon, principal of the consulting agency Figure 8 Thinking, director of the strategic design MBA program at Philadelphia University, and a facilitator at the Half The Sky Leadership Institute. When it comes to speaking with confidence during presentations, Natalie says, "This is one of the things that I find myself counseling my senior-level fashion management students whom I teach at an undergraduate level. They tend to be mainly women and they also tend to speak with that 'up speak' at the end of their sentences, where it sounds like they have a question every time they say something. I always remind them that you can't go into industries speaking that way if you want to be taken seriously. You have to make declarative statements and speak in sentences that end with a period."

Part and parcel of that presence is how you "present," at meetings, during conference calls, and in both formal and informal presentations where you're called upon to provide succinct information in a meaningful and understandable way. I can't stress enough how critical this skill is, not only to executive presence but to leadership as well.

In a variety of ways, in dozens of applications, you have to be able to rapidly synthesize an idea, present it to a group of people, and provide feedback. If you are uncomfortable with speaking in public, joining Toastmasters or practicing skills with your boss or another mentor are critical for achieving success.

Dressing for the Job You Want

There is no denying that one of the critical factors of executive presence is dressing for the part. Of course, your knowledge, performance, skill set, and energy all contribute greatly to your executive presence. But unfortunately, women are judged on how we dress. Think of wardrobe as the key to the door that gets you into the right room.

Research shows that depending on your work environment, your appearance can help you get opportunities, and it can help you miss out on them too. Never underestimate its importance. Remember, books, seminars, articles, and workshops exist solely to discuss appearance—what and what *not* to wear.

Again, not every organization is the same. Some companies thrive on diversity; they welcome employees with unconventional appearances. Still, in most corporate environments, the onus is on women to look, act, and dress a certain way. This requires many of us to make compromises.

I know I am judged because I am a larger woman. I have to be aware of how I am dressed when I show up. The same goes for younger women or even petite women who may be judged because of their appearance. Women who dress in a manner that is considered provocative are judged harshly as well. Clothes that are too tight or too short may make an impression that distracts people from what you want to say about yourself. Many of the women who come through Half The Sky programs find that after they improve their outward appearance, people begin to treat them differently.

The key is finding a look that works both for you and the environment you work in. Once you hit on an appearance that is both comfortable and appropriate for the workplace, you can then concentrate on the perhaps bigger issues that go hand in hand with your appearance to create a strong, brand-conscious executive presence. Body language, posture, eye contact, a firm handshake, and energy—these factors all affect our brand. Maybe they shouldn't matter, but they do.

How you dress and carry yourself communicates a message to your company, your clients, and your peers about how you feel. Dressing for the job you want and being appropriate for your environment signals to others you are confident in yourself. As a size 20, I often say, "If you can't hide it, decorate it." Create an image that enhances and communicates your best self.

Each of us has a brand in the workplace that's part and parcel of our professional reputation. In every encounter, scenario, presentation, task force, and team meeting, this brand is being formed and reformed, reinforced, and reevaluated. It all leads to one thing: your executive presence.

Making an Appearance: Executive Presence, Gravitas, and You

You have a workplace presence, whether or not you know it, understand it, or acknowledge it. According to Sylvia Ann Hewlett, the author of *Executive Presence: The Missing Link Between Merit and Success* (HarperBusiness, 2014), "Executive presence will not earn you promotion after promotion, but lack of executive presence will impede your ability to get as far as you want to go. Quite simply," she adds, "promotions are not just functions of ability, values, or the numbers you hit, but also rest critically on how you are perceived."

Gravitas alone won't make you a leader, nor will communication or appearance if they exist in isolation. But together, all three create an executive presence that's hard to ignore and even harder to deny. Since we've already addressed gravitas, let's move down the list to appearance and discuss how the way you look affects your rate of success.

As I've said, it's important to dress appropriately for the environment in which you work. I don't care what's written in the employee manual. Every company has a dress code—written or unwritten—and it might not be readily apparent until you're actually working there.

Take note and study what the other woman leaders are wearing, what looks best, and who is the best dressed. Determine how you can best merge your personal style with the workplace dress code.

When it comes to appearance, here are the kinds of things that can trip women up:

o Skirts, pants, or tops that are too tight, too loose, or otherwise inappropriate

o Bra straps or panty lines showing

o Clothes that are too provocative or revealing

o Heels that are great for a club but not appropriate for the work environment

o Hairstyles or hair colors that are too flamboyant and/or too conservative

I don't want to make it sound like appearance is the most important factor. In fact, none of these factors alone—influence, skills, ability to present, appearance, or grit—can on its own define your personal brand. Here's the thing: If you don't get your appearance right, it's a distraction, and nobody will listen to what you have to say. Think of your appearance as the keys to the car. You won't go anywhere if the keys don't fit.

However, the more appropriate your appearance is for the workplace, the less of an issue it becomes. If your personal brand boils down to your being "the blonde with the short skirts," then yes, that factor is dominating how people perceive you. And it probably won't reflect well on how you communicate or show up.

Showing Up in Style

Make no mistake: You are judged on your appearance. At 56 years of age, I am, by all standards, overweight and a size 18–20. At one time in my career, I weighed more than 380 pounds and was a size 4X.

No matter what my weight, however, I worked really hard to dress well, and I was always well groomed. I also wore the best clothes I could afford and did whatever it took to make myself as stylish and polished as possible, because I knew when I walked into the room the first thing that people were going to think was "fat." The other perceptions people have about plus-size women tend to include "stupid," "sloppy," "lazy," and "incompetent." None of these perceptions are positive.

Now, my health is important to me and I have worked hard to lose weight and shape up over the years. But I still have a long way to go. I share that with you because these were some of the barriers I had to push out of my way each and every time I walked into a room. I had to enter with my head held high, my shoulders back, making eye contact and with an executive presence that matched or exceeded that of everyone else there. I had to have the full package—communication, appearance, and gravitas—despite what I looked like. I had to cross that barrier with every single person who met me for the first time.

In our program at Half The Sky, we have women who come in who do not look like executives. Their internal competence and their external appearance are incongruent. It affects their overall presence and weakens their brand—not because they are being unfairly judged but because their appearance is part of the message they're sending. If it's unprofessional, it says, "If I am not taking care of myself, then I am not going to take care of your company, either."

We also see women who are uncomfortable with their body type. They appear, for lack of a better term, "sloppy." In one case, after our second session, once we felt a little more comfortable with each other, I asked a woman about her clothing. She told me that she was "not feeling very good" about herself.

Politely but firmly, I told her she didn't look polished or put together and I worried about whether or not people would engage with her. She took the words to heart, went out, invested in some new clothes, and, the next time I saw her, looked like a completely different person. She told me that her boss mentioned how good she looked and she asked him why he hadn't said anything to her about her appearance before. He replied that "he didn't know how to mention" it to her. This example just goes to show that people are quietly judging you even if they don't say so.

One thing I try to share with the women I work with is that when you feel good about yourself, appearance becomes a habit, not a special event. In other words, you don't just dress nicely when the big boss is coming, but you look forward to looking professional in every circumstance because you know the value of your personal brand. For better or worse, how you look affects how you show up, so it's important to show up in a way that is both professional and appropriate for you.

How to Shine Your Own Light: Five Tips for Showing Up Strong

I have a client—we'll call her Terry—who perfectly embodies this unwillingness to self-promote, often at her own expense.

For instance, every time Terry gets in front of her board of directors, she plummets. One reason is that she doesn't really have strong relationships with the board, so she goes in cold and gets more and more uncomfortable as the meeting progresses. Any criticism, either real or perceived, makes her feel under attack and she is instantly on the defensive.

As a result, she really doesn't show up well at these meetings. She is also what you would call a "direct" leader, and we all know how men—particularly groups of men—respond to that! She often wondered if she should adjust her style for these meetings, but we dug deeper to see if there was anything that she was overlooking in terms of results.

Ultimately, Terry realized she wasn't collecting enough metrics when she was preparing for these meetings. If the CFO drilled down on something she wasn't prepared for, her default reaction was to get flustered and emotional.

Terry did her homework, demanding more accurate and timely information, and she was able to provide the board with the data members wanted. Now that she's better prepared, she's cooler, calmer, and more collected before, during, and after these board meetings. We also worked to adjust her personal brand at these meetings and elsewhere in the organization. We talked about her leadership style in the context of a lamp with a dimmer switch: Sometimes, depending on your environment, you don't need the 100-watt bulb. You can use the dimmer switch to raise and lower your energy and power as needed.

If you or someone you know is struggling with workplace brand, consider my Five Tips for Showing Up Strong:

1. *Put together a package that's right for the environment.* There is no blank template I can give you for putting together a smart, sophisticated, professional package that will wow your

workplace. That's basically because, now more than ever, the workplace dynamic is shifting. While one corporate culture may, in fact, covet the smart, sophisticated look, another (say at an advertising agency, computer game company, or software startup) may embrace funky, spiky hair and tattoos. What I can tell you is that, while you can never go wrong being yourself, it also never hurts to fit into the environment—within reason. The package *does* matter. Having a strong executive presence and appearance is what helps you get a seat at the table. Not focusing on this sends negative messages to leaders and clients and will keep you from getting to the next level.

2. *Build your network.* Building a strong network is important in order to develop relationships with people at all levels of the organization. This gives you a "safety net" of people who can give you deadlines, deliverables, and guardrails around what does and doesn't work in the organization. Some might call that mentoring, but this is a less formal and more populated form of getting exposure and learning at the same time.

3. *Conduct an internal audit.* It's also important to know your strengths, so you can capitalize on them, but also having a strong sense of your lack of ability or skills in certain areas so that you can shore those things up. You can build confidence by exploring what your skills are via an honest, sincere, and thorough internal audit. Develop those skills, one by one, until you have more confidence around them—and in general.

4. *Know your tolerance for risk.* It's important to know how comfortable you are with risk so that you can gradually start moving beyond your comfort zone. Risk taking is important because not only does it build your confidence; it also helps you grow as a leader. In many of my speaking engagements, I show

a video of a young girl on top of a mountain. She asks her ski instructor how far it is down. She is obviously terrified at the top of the mountain, and as she skis down you hear her screaming. But when she gets to the bottom, you see her shadow posed as if to say, "Oh, that was nothing!"

5. *Recognize that fear is a liar.* As you build your confidence, you can step outside your comfort zone and accomplish things you never thought were possible. When we don't take risks, we allow our fear to paralyze us. Fear is a liar. It robs us of opportunity, of advancement, and, above all, of confidence. Taking risks helps us to combat and, eventually, master the negative self-talk that keeps so many women right where they are. Dawn Callahan, CMO of Boingo Wireless, whom we met in the Introduction, tells us, "One of the most important lessons I've learned is that everybody feels terrified. And so when you realize that, 'Oh my God, everybody is in the exact same scenario,' it really takes the power out of it."

Obviously, if these things were all you had to do to build confidence, I'd be concluding this book rather than just warming up! But these tips are a great "starter kit" for working on your confidence right here, right now.

Profile in Confidence:
Jill Campbell, Executive Vice President and Chief Operations Officer, Cox Communications

When I think about confidence, I think about energy and excitement. You can feel it in the room when somebody walks in. And if somebody's not excited about what they're doing or being, it shows pretty readily. It manifests itself in the way you walk in a room: You've got a smile on your face, a firm handshake, and a great pair of shoes—because packaging is important. I think for women it's even more important than for men. Don't underestimate the first impression. I make sure when I talk to young women not to just assume that they can pull whatever they want out of their closet and go. This is part of their leadership profile. And if you look good, then it helps you feel more confident as well.

I had a mentor and colleague named May Douglas, who was our chief people officer, and when I started in a corporate role, she said, "You have to dress up. The guys may be wearing khakis, but as women, in order to be taken more seriously and look the part, you need to dress like a leader." At first, I wasn't quite sure what that meant, but when I watched her and other powerful women, I started to realize that you can't just throw anything on or something you'd wear out for dinner. It's a very deliberate presentation that you have to make.

I think that the most important thing you can do to build confidence is to be the expert at what you are there for. You have a right to be there. You wouldn't be in the room unless people knew that you were the right person for the role, so you've got to start there and dig deep in and say to yourself, "Okay, sister, I have the right to be here," and you know, dig deep to get that, because you're not going to get that internally. So I—I think it just goes back to . . . you can practice, I mean clearly. But you have to know what it is you're trying to say and what values you're bringing to the conversation and why you're in the room to begin with.

If I feel really nervous in front of a group and I'm unsure or uncomfortable, I've got the little naysayer in my head

going "Why are you here? They're not going to accept you."
Then I just kick that voice in the teeth and I say, "No!" to
that voice! "I am good at this," I tell it. And then I remember
those times when I felt really confident and I just put that
back on. So it's a lot of positive talk to help you to feel that
way. It's confidence self-talk.

Counting on Communication

In addition to gravitas and appearance, two other factors that
affect your executive presence are your written and verbal
communications. Ask yourself: How well do you convey your
messages across multiple platforms, including in person, on
conference calls, one-on-one, and in groups? Also, are you able
to synthesize information effectively, accurately, and concisely?
Basically, are you someone who is able to articulate an idea to
others? While appearance and gravitas are prime leadership real
estate, don't neglect communication in your climb to the top.

One of the biggest gaps for people as they try to move up
in their careers is their ability to present and speak. In our program, we help women to become better presenters. The training
touches on everything from the materials that they use to their
physical presentations. One critical focus is voice. How you use
your voice matters significantly.

When you speak in a particularly high-pitched voice, you
begin to irritate others and lose your credibility. It doesn't matter
what you're saying; if folks can hear only a certain tone, you are
no longer communicating effectively. Sometimes what we say is
perfectly credible, but *how* we say it loses credibility through the
pitch of our voice or an impatient, snide, or rude tone.

If your voice runs high when presenting, or it sounds like
you're asking questions when you're actually making a statement,

consider picturing a period at the end of each sentence. If you're too loud or too soft, moderate your tone so that it sounds more even-keeled. If you're speaking too fast, slow it down. If you put an "um" between sentences, learn to stop. All of these affectations impact your presentation. As we've found in our program, these small adjustments can work wonders.

Lily Kelly-Radford of LEAP Leadership, whom we met earlier, explains, "It is important for women not to give their power away by the use of voice inflection. Women will often singsong their comments, and they will likely, in the earlier stages of their career, use an uptick in their voice tone at the end of a sentence, which almost poses it as a question. A voice punctuates just like grammar, and a sentence has punctuation. It's a period at the end."

If you don't think of yourself as an effective communicator, or if you have received feedback along those lines, consider taping yourself and listening to how you actually sound. Then, if you find it as grating as everyone else seems to, try to make some adjustments. When nervous, we often sound different than when we're relaxed, so it may simply be an issue of feeling more comfortable with the material, or even ourselves, that helps to conquer our pitch problems.

Also, watch how you comport yourself when communicating, whether one-on-one or in groups. Consider whether or not your body language is appropriate for the situation. When in doubt, record yourself or have a trusted friend or mentor record you. Seeing ourselves as others see us can help us present more effectively.

Our brands are affected by how we present ourselves. One way to have more executive presence is not to be overly apologetic. It's certainly appropriate to own up to our mistakes every so often, but . . . all the time? A lot of women dismiss their abilities in small ways that send a big message: *"This may be a stupid question, but . . . "* or *"This might not be important, but . . . "*

When a woman leads off with this sort of negative disclaimer, which is often an unconscious habit, it affects how people view her opinions and suggestions. Instead of stating something confidently and owning it, this person has effectively negated her own idea. Now no one has to give it any credence. Basically, she dug a hole and threw her own suggestion deep down inside—and now she's wondering why no one considers it seriously!

Lily Kelly-Radford explains, "Because confidence is a little more complicated and involves a lot of variables, I don't think some of those variables can be faked, but I do believe others can be faked. I think you can sort of practice assertiveness. I think you can practice posture, which is part of what exudes confidence. I think you can practice pacing until it becomes natural. And I think you can practice certain speaking skills, as well as certain elements of appearance. But, beyond that, the portion of confidence that can't be faked would be the gravitas, which often comes with facing certain things that are difficult for you and working through them, as well as some level of experience that people often feel they don't have."

So strengthening your executive presence would include checking your appearance as well as making sure you're showing the style that matches the leadership position to which you're aspiring. What are the prevalent styles in the organization? If it's conservative, for example, you have to be cognizant of that and, to some extent, mirror it in how you look, talk, and act.

This may not be your personal style every day, but some compromise is necessary to fit your personal brand into the organizational style. Personally, I don't wear suits, but I do wear colors that both blend into the office flow and mark my personal style.

You have to be aware of what the workplace considers appropriate. Again, it might not be your own personal style, but see how you can blend styles to fit in while feeling comfortable and true to yourself. If you're a younger woman, in particular, you are better served by seeing how others dress first and erring on the side of caution. Then, as you grow more comfortable with the appropriate work style, you can begin to add your own style, accessories, or flair to it. But do so gradually.

One woman I worked with—an attractive, fit blonde in her 30s—used to dress older than her age. For a long time she wouldn't even show off her arms in the workplace. It turned out that her leader was very conservative. Now, however, she is in a new and different environment where she has much more creative freedom—and she is still user-appropriate. She wears more colors and often arrives at work in a sleeveless dress with a suit jacket. In the summer, she exposes her arms. She's still very conservative—perhaps a holdover from her previous job—but she's more stylish in her new environment. She just had to adapt.

And so do you.

The Takeaway

Executive presence is both a state of mind and a state of being. The whole world can see how we look, how we communicate, and how we act. But internally, our confidence tends to determine all of those factors.

When it comes to executive presence, Sara King says, "We really have to grow and diversify our experiences. At the same time, continuing to own and develop an expertise and to not let go of that says you create even more value."

It's as though there's a magic formula that increases as we exhibit more confidence. Putting on your version of a power suit, standing straight, looking people in the eye, having a strong handshake—all of these behaviors tell the world that you have your "mojo" going. The more confident I am—the more I raise my hand, the more conversations I join, and the more people who see me doing it—the more opportunities I will have. That's why executive presence is such a powerful branding tool: With it, you all but scream leadership potential.

Without it, most people won't hear you at all.

One of the things I try to tell people, women in particular, is that you can't fake executive presence. As Sophia A. Nelson says, "I don't agree with 'Fake it till you make it.' It is an old mantra. It is one that particularly women like to throw around. And faking it is really part of the problem for us as women, because most of the time that's exactly what we do. We're inauthentic, we wear a mask, lying not only to others, but very much to ourselves."

Over the course of our careers, we will be held to some very real standards. It's not a matter of "you either have it, or you don't," because as we've seen in this chapter, with confidence, with accomplishments, and with persistence, you can steadily gain executive presence. But along the way, not everything is a "fake it till you make it" issue. You must act authentically, in a way that feels comfortable for you, and yet puts your best foot forward.

According to the Girl Scouts' Natalye Paquin, "No one likes a phony. People will kind of smoke you out when you're not being authentic. And it's really taxing, and it draws on your energy if you just can't be yourself. And so I would say just be your authentic self, because that's the person who you know, who will be with you in the long run. And it doesn't mean that you can't grow, or that you have to stay the same. I'm not suggesting that at all. But, you know, you either grow or die. But just be true to who you are."

Your outward appearance does affect how people respond to you, and first impressions (good and bad) can be powerful. Why not make sure you are appropriate and authentic? You can be who you are and still have a polished, professional, and pulled-together manner. I know that when I meet people they are expecting a CEO-level executive. A local client of mine told me that she was always impressed by how I looked when she bumped into me around Philadelphia.

If that means systematically improving your wardrobe, do it. It doesn't cost a lot of money to wear clothes that advertise your brand in a positive and confident way. Many stores offer free shopper/stylist services, or you might consider asking for the assistance of someone in your network who always looks great. Feeling comfortable in your own skin and losing the critical voice we often use when we talk about ourselves goes a long way in exuding a positive executive presence.

Profile in Confidence:
Ines Temple, CEO and President of Lee Hecht Harrison, Peru

"Here are some tips for women to exhibit confidence. First of all, we should walk straight, occupy all the space that truly belongs to us (which should be plenty), and learn to smile while speaking. I truly believe charisma and charm are both key to being perceived as a warm person and that's key in generating trust. Confidence is about generating trust more than trying to impress others by our knowledge or intelligence. If people trust you, then the relationships work and you can start doing your job. Also, being natural and treating everyone the same, while being positive, works wonders to gain people's good will, acceptance, and approval. Once we give that to people, by reciprocity we will get it back. It works beautifully, but we should do this first."

4

Coaching—and Being Coached

This chapter addresses one of the most intense and beneficial relationships to exist in any workplace: the one that results from being coached and coaching others. This one-on-one, win/win relationship improves the lives of both participants, creating a "circle of influence" that makes coaches out of those being coached, and helps us help others in return. The key here is being committed to self-improvement and open to feedback and guidance. You will always hold the map, but a good coach is someone who holds the light for you. Coaching is another important tool in developing your confidence.

Coaching for Success

We all have areas in our lives and our professions that need a little buttressing from time to time. It might be technology, social media, marketing, public speaking, or appearance—even playing well with others. All too often, perhaps out of a vague fear of being perceived as "needy" if they seek out help, women go it on their own and either try to "fix" these problems for themselves or simply neglect them outright.

I can tell you from experience there is no weakness in trying to better ourselves, whether through classes, seminars, books, or, in this case, being coached. Leaders want those who are willing to seek help and get it in order to better themselves. I've watched both myself and countless others find success on both sides of the coaching desk—being coached and coaching others.

Being Coached

If you've ever wanted direct, one-on-one assistance in solving a problem or learning a skill, coaching could be right up your alley. There may be coaches in your organization; there are also professional coaches who, for a fee, delve into whatever skill set you're seeking to possess and make sure that you get it.

Regardless of which type of coach fits your personal style and budget, here are some things you definitely want to find in a qualified coach:

○ *Expertise.* You want to find a coach with expertise in the skill set you want to acquire—a coach who can help you turn a weakness into a strength. If social media is your weakness, then find a social media expert. If public speaking is your Achilles' heel, find a great public speaker, and so on. There's simply no sense in going through the exercise and the expense of being coached by someone who's hardly any better at a skill than you are!

o *Availability*. Obviously, timing is everything. If someone doesn't have the time to coach you, then no matter how ideal she might have been, it's simply not meant to be. Move on and find another coach. Or, if possible, you might be able to wait until the desired coach's availability opens up.

o *Accessibility*. Your coach may be available, but is she accessible? In other words, will it be convenient for you to visit with her?

o *Affordability*. If this is not a volunteer or mentor relationship, can you afford this coach? Coaches come in all shapes, sizes, and price ranges, and there's no sense breaking the bank to gain a skill if it's going to take you years to dig out from the expense. Coaching should be an open, honest, and enjoyable experience, but it's hard to enjoy yourself, let alone learn something, if you're constantly worrying about what something—or someone—costs.

o *Compatibility*. Finally, are you compatible? No matter how great, expert, or successful a coach may be, if you simply don't like him, don't get along with him, or don't feel comfortable with him, chances are it's not going to be a successful relationship, let alone an enjoyable experience.

A good coach can help you identify very specific strategies to get over your hurdle. The critical factor is that you are open to self-exploration and to feedback. As you can see, coaching is an intimate relationship—and personal collaboration—so finding the right one is critical for your success.

Now let's see how you might benefit from coaching others.

Coaching Others

When you coach others, you form an intense bond with another professional—whether in or out of your industry—and you tend to benefit from the coaching experience as well. Just as teachers learn from every class and student, coaches grow and learn from the process.

Having personally coached dozens of folks, I always walk away from the experience with either a new perspective, a new skill set, or in some cases simply a new enthusiasm for the job I'm doing or want to do.

It's easy to get into a rut in our work, to find a groove and stay there, with little interaction outside the safe confines of our office, team, or floor. But coaching another professional—who is typically either younger or at least junior to you—helps bring you out of your comfort zone and form a strong bond with a like-minded individual.

One thing that's so refreshing about coaching is that people who want to get coached are almost always enthusiastic, energetic go-getters who make you see what you do in new and interesting ways. This can have positive benefits for you as well as for the person you're coaching.

Often, I find myself brushing up on topics I've let get a little, shall we say, "dusty" in my current role, all in an effort to provide the best coaching experience possible for the other person. This helps me as well as the person I'm coaching as I get reacquainted with the skill and learn to use it in new and interesting ways.

I highly recommend coaching others as a way to "pay it forward" as you grow and reach in your career. As far as relationships go, coaching is both as intimate and as beneficial as it gets. There have been numerous times when someone I coached went on to do quite well and in return shared a little of that spotlight and success with me.

In short, never underestimate the power of grace, charity, or professional generosity. Natalie Nixon, whom we met in Chapter 3, says, "A term that I've started using is 'professionally generous.' And these are women who go out of their way to be helpful, to be a connector, to be a sponsor, and it's without any type of provocation and they expect nothing in return. And it indicates to me that they have a high level of confidence. They don't feel threatened. They feel they have an understanding that they got to where they are because of someone who was professionally generous and gracious to them. And it has this kind of pay-it-forward effect."

The Takeaway

Coaching is a worthwhile and intimate collaboration that I highly recommend. One of the most appealing aspects of coaching is its one-on-one nature. This means that you can only do it to a certain extent, and only so often, making it a very limited role that you—or your coach—can play. This puts "guardrails" around how much time you can coach others or be coached. Indeed, these are very special and exclusive relationships.

Profile in Confidence:
Susan Jin Davis, Senior Vice President, Comcast

As with most things in life, when it comes to confidence, practice makes perfect. So initially I do think that you have to fake it 'til you make it until it really sticks. Confidence is an iterative and cumulative phenomenon. As you practice confidence repeatedly, you gain more actual confidence. As you build up those experiences of acting confidently, you eventually become truly confident.

However, I also believe that having a foundation of confidence is essential. Knowing yourself, accepting yourself, being comfortable in your skin are the baselines of true confidence. Lack of confidence comes from being insecure and self-conscious—that arises from self-doubt, fear of failure, and worrying about what others think of you. As you get more experience, you get strength from within, not without. And that propels you into the land of confidence. Being courageous and having true grit and taking risks are also foundational. And most importantly, when you feel loved, you can do anything…at least you feel that way and that's confidence.

I was taught by my mother from an early age to have a "thick face"—never let them see you sweat. But eventually I convinced myself I belonged at the table, I deserved to be here, and then it no longer became just a tough face but who I was. Also the self-consciousness falls away over the years. After a while you say, the hell with them/it: I'm me and that ain't going to change no matter what you think. If you have that attitude, what others think about you just doesn't matter as much. You're charging through that door, over that wall, around that blockade without hesitation. And if that doesn't work, you keep trying. Failure becomes part of the process of getting better at what you do.

5

Building Your IPO (Information, Power, and Opportunity)

In the real world, IPO stands for initial public offering. It's the first sale of a company's stock to the general public. However, as discussed in Chapter 1, my definition of IPO—information, power, and opportunity—explains how these three integral values play a huge part in the relationships we form at every juncture of our careers.

Information

Information is a key resource that fuels both power and opportunity. Information comes in many forms, including:

o Which companies are hiring

o Which companies are firing

o Who's just moved where

o Who just got hired

o Who just got fired

o What trends are hot

o Which trends are not

As you can see, information is fuel for successful people. Personally, I can never get enough!

Power

I have to reemphasize that in the case of relationships, the term *power* does not refer to how high you can rise but how strong your relationships can be. In IPO, power is the link between knowledge—*what* you know—and opportunity—*who* you know. Power is that sweet spot where knowledge and opportunity meet. The more knowledge you have—about what's going on, why, where, when, and who's involved—the more powerful you become.

Your power lies not just in how you can help yourself but in how you can help others as well. In fact, the more you help others, the more powerful you become. This is the "secret sauce" to networking and relationships: By connecting with others, you help them help you.

For example, let's say a former intern, employee, colleague, or acquaintance checks in with you to let you know she's left the corporate world to open up shop as a freelance graphic designer. You have a pleasant chat, file the information away, and move on with your day.

Later in the week, or month, or even year, you hear from another colleague who is starting up a new software company and, in an effort to keep costs down, needs a freelance graphic designer for game cover art, posters, and web graphics. You put the two together, they make wonderful magic, and everyone's happy.

So, how does this help you become more powerful? Simple: Happy, grateful people never forget what you've done for them. Like I said, it may be years in the offing, but eventually, I may get a request to speak at that friend's software company, which now employs hundreds of people. Or he may refer me to someone who needs a speaker for an upcoming management conference. Not to mention, one day I may need to call on my graphic designer friend for a rush job.

As you continue to connect, meet, and network with new people, your power will grow exponentially. Each new contact brings with her both knowledge and—the most powerful ally of all—opportunity.

Opportunity

The best relationships represent a mutual, or shared, opportunity. Take my former intern whom I told you about earlier, who is now in the sports industry. As he continues to grow and succeed in his field, he may one day reach out to me for advice on how to become a thought leader in his industry.

I think we all agree that branding ourselves in our company is worthwhile, but so is marketing ourselves as thought leaders in our field, in or outside of the organization. My presence on LinkedIn represents an attempt to steer my online brand toward potential contacts and relationships. I may, in fact, have once worked with a sports magazine editor who may be able to help my friend grow his name, expertise, and prestige in the sports world. Perhaps my sports guy ends up writing a great article for this editor, one that becomes so popular that it turns into a column, which makes both of these friends very happy. And it makes me a powerful ally in their continued success.

This represents an opportunity for me because, as I blog and write and publish, it's often helpful to network among other editors, authors, writers, bloggers, and columnists, be it to seek feedback, support, knowledge, a blurb for a new book, or an introduction to a certain editor.

This is just one simple, and admittedly narrow, example of the many opportunities that present themselves with each contact and each relationship. Think of the people you already know. How can they help you? And how can you help them? Now, multiply that by every new person you meet, relate to, and remember. That's the power of opportunity; it's the difference between managing and leading, between surviving and thriving—between failure and success.

The Takeaway

Everyone's IPO is different, and the mix is always in flux and flow. For instance, you may experience a period in your career where you're in the process of gathering information. Consequently, you don't have much power to wield or opportunities to take advantage of at this particular time. At other junctures, you may be taking advantage of so many opportunities that you neglect the information gathering.

In general, though, as you become comfortable with the trifecta that is your IPO, all three components—information, power, and opportunity—will be in balance to ensure that your most positive relationships will also be your most powerful.

PART TWO

Reputation

*Begin somewhere. You cannot build a
reputation on what you intend to do.*
—Liz Smith, journalist

Think of your reputation as the echo that lingers in the room long after you leave. In fact, it's also what precedes you into the room, a kind of subconscious energy or presence you carry around with you wherever you go. For me, "reputation" and "brand" are nearly interchangeable. Each is a reflection of your executive leadership presence.

Many people think they know what their reputations are. Some are absolutely right, while others are *way* off base. What people in the organization actually think about us is important because it affects how they make decisions about us. It can even affect how much exposure we're getting in the organization and whether or not people want to sponsor us for various leadership opportunities that arise.

If you have a reputation as a dependable, trustworthy, and discreet person, then people are far more willing to share information, access, and opportunities. If you develop a reputation as someone with fickle allegiances and loyalties, or with a mean streak, then you may find opportunities closed off to you.

Reputations don't exist in a vacuum. Quite often, the way we are perceived—our personal brand—is tied into our relationship with others and how *they* are perceived. We need to be careful about the workplace alliances we make and be sure that they are advantageous to our brand as well as our career.

Many leaders are afraid to know how they are actually perceived. They rarely get feedback from their bosses on areas where they need to improve, especially the higher up they move in the organization. Yet, it is vitally important that they know how they are viewed if they are to continue improving and growing. We implemented an assessment tool in our Half The Sky Leadership program for this very reason: to give the participant feedback from her direct supervisor and to open up the lines of communication. For many women, this was the first time they received professional feedback.

Profile in Confidence:
Lisa Chang, SVP Human Resources, AMB Group LLC
(Atlanta Falcons, MLS Atlanta, New Atlanta Stadium, PGA Tour Superstores)

When thinking about how we show up, I have a story: I was in a desk product management position where we had some big project. We were trying to figure out the answer to the question "How do we do the sales and the distributions and do we do X or do we do Y?" I was fairly new into the stint and I must have stayed up all weekend trying to solve what I thought was a mathematical problem.

At the end of the weekend, I suddenly realized that there really was no answer; it was merely degrees of right or wrong. There was nothing as simple as "It's A and then B." It was "If you do A, you have to give up on that; if you do B, you have to give up on that; and the question is, which do you want more of, A or B?"

It took me all weekend to realize that I didn't know the answer, because I didn't have the experience and I didn't know where we were. And I remember saying to my husband that weekend, "I am totally going to get fired. I am going to go in there and they are going to think, 'Okay, what the heck have we done? We put this person in charge and she has no clue.'" But I thought, "If it's meant to be, it's meant to be, and if you can't do it then it's better for them to know now, right?"

So, I go in with my analysis and I basically tell the CEO, "Actually, there is no right answer. I have sliced and diced it a million different ways and there really is no A or B. The question is: What is more important and how do we prioritize, you know, what do we do?"

I was expecting her to say "You are an idiot," but instead she just looked at me and she said, "That's exactly what I have been struggling with and I appreciate you admitting that because, I honestly expected you to come in with an answer. This just validates the struggle that we are having and so now we can all focus on deciding what is more important, A or B." It was a huge relief, because I really thought for sure I was getting fired.

I think when you feel you are making a mistake or you don't have the answers, just admit that. If I think about almost every situation where you are trying to build a reputation, or credibility, or a relationship with anyone from a business standpoint, it is always about making that person feel there is a mutual best interest involved.

If you are overconfident, there are times when the other party may feel "Well, that person is not really looking out for my best interest," and that can be a real turnoff. Whereas someone who is truly comfortable and confident can come and talk about how the relationship can be mutually beneficial. How the work relationship can progress, what we can do for you, what you can do for us, here is my experience, I have this, and you have that. It's a series of balancing compromises.

So, I think having a lot of confidence also means making that person feel comfortable. Because remember, perception is reality and so while I might feel I might have confidence, if the other person perceives me to be overconfident, then I have just shot myself in the foot. Whereas, it is my job to make sure that that person feels comfortable with me and you have to have that emotional intelligence to the audience to know. Because what confidence might look to one person is arrogance to another, so you really have to be able to read your audience.

The Takeaway

As we move forward through the next section, think critically about your own brand and how eager people are to work with you. If your brand needs fixing, you will find tools here for that. And even if your brand is already strong, you will find tools to help you make it even stronger.

6

Seize Opportunities with Courageous Leadership

Who are you and how do you lead? These will be two defining questions surrounding your reputation at work, and ones that most women find confusing simply because they don't ask them of themselves. In this chapter, I will explore the topic of courageous leadership and help you discover how to seize opportunities you might normally not consider or even be afraid to consider.

Courageous Leadership

A lack of confidence or belief in ourselves can keep us from telling the truth, taking a risk, or raising our hands. Having a true sense of our own moral and ethical compass and a willingness to stand our ground when necessary is something that can embolden us.

Naturally, being courageous isn't necessarily something that junior leaders have the opportunity to do. Instead, they're too busy doing the work they are assigned and just trying to get the lay of the land as they climb the career ladder. But remember: Knowledge is power, and knowing the power of courage can help build a strong foundation for future leadership decisions and opportunities.

At a higher level, senior executives may struggle with leading courageously when they have to talk about difficult topics. In my experience, it often comes down to "truth telling." Courageous leaders are the ones who are willing to tell people what they need to hear, even if it's unpopular. As you take this on, keep in mind that diplomacy is key to maintaining your good reputation. There's a critical difference between being a truth teller and simply being negative.

According to Jill Campbell, "If you're invited to the table, you have the right to be there, so speak up. If people think you're being aggressive, you have to figure out the tone in which you're giving the message. So, you don't interrupt people, you don't do all those things you see the guys in the board room doing, but you know, quietly get your message out there just the same."

Today, courageous leadership is more a necessity than a luxury. Every organization has room for improvement, and many are in real danger of imploding if someone doesn't step up and be a truth teller. Whether they're big truths or small ones, they must come from you. Tell the truth, but be diplomatic, knowing that in many cases you may be talking to the person who is, or represents, the problem. For instance, perhaps you're in a meeting and someone says, "That's impossible!" You may need to be the person who says, "I understand the challenges seem insurmountable right now, but could we think about this differently?" Or even, "I understand your position on this, but can I invite you to consider this other option?" Such responses politely but firmly refute the idea of impossibility and offer another option for surmounting the challenge, perhaps in a new and unique way.

When you feel strongly about something, courageous leadership defines how you bring that to the forefront. We're likely to overstep when we feel the most passionate, but courageous leaders know to temper passion with reason for a skeptical audience. What's more, courageous leaders often get shot down by less courageous higher-ups. Yet even when your ideas are brushed aside, it's still courageous to be able to say to yourself, "I have stated my case and brought my idea forward. That's as much as I can do given my position or status in the company."

Leading Courageously Is Not the Same as Leading Carelessly—or Even Cruelly

Courageous leadership is not about telling people that they are always wrong. They're often wrong, especially when they care less than you do. But leading courageously is about offering solutions, not scolding people. More important, it's about stating the cases that may be unpopular, but being willing to take a stand when people say that you're wrong.

I remember being in a meeting of senior-level people once and making a statement about how I felt concerning a topic that was being discussed. The head of the organization vehemently and vocally disagreed with me. My boss at the time didn't back me up but took me aside and warned me to tread lightly.

Through it all, I felt strongly that I was correct. Even though I felt outnumbered and outgunned, I firmly but very respectfully stayed my course. I recall saying, "I am respectfully disagreeing with you and here is why . . . " Despite my making a clear and logical case, the senior executive still felt he was right, and it was understood that our disagreement was going to impact not only our relationship but perhaps my position as well. But still, I stood my ground. He looked me in the eye and I didn't break eye contact. He said something to the effect that we would move on to another topic.

It was uncomfortable and it didn't help matters that he was new to the organization. I could feel my face getting red. After the meeting, however, we continued our conversation. I knew I still needed to stand my ground and also needed to be respectful. But at some point I also had to stop pushing.

I was very respectful in what I said and how I said it, but through it all I did not acquiesce. I stayed the course. Had I been more junior in my career, even though I might have felt the same way, I might not have had enough credibility to do that. I might have brought it up once and when I felt the mood in the room going south, said, "okay, okay," and stopped. But I tell the story now because it's not just about being courageous for the sake of being courageous. Truly courageous leadership involves taking the temperature of the room and assessing how strong your reputation is in the current situation to determine how far to push an idea or opinion.

You also have to know what your relationship is with the people in the room. I was pretty senior in the company at the time, so I knew I had enough credibility to stand up and hold my ground. I also knew that this executive was going to more seriously consider whatever I had to say after that because of the way I presented my case: factually and rationally.

The Takeaway

Be a courageous leader. Let others know you are passionate about the organization, your role in it, and how you can help. Brand yourself as someone who speaks up with confidence and competence, so that you are never caught unprepared. Courage is not about having to be right. It's about making sure the right conversations are being held at the right time, in the right way. If you are more junior in your career, it's important to weigh and measure your comments but not be afraid to speak your mind, share an idea, or ask questions.

7

Recognizing Your Own Abilities

One aspect of being competent but not confident is under-selling, even underappreciating, our own personal skills as they relate to our brand or reputation. Perhaps because we feel we can't be our true selves at work, we neglect to offer the intense value inherent in what we alone can bring to the work-place equation.

Competence, Confidence, and the "Click"

The big message in all of this is what I call the *click*, which is when a woman's confidence and competence connect to each other and serve her well. At Half The Sky as well as in my coach-ing practice, I work with women who are not newcomers in their careers; they have been working for 10 or 15 years and they don't suffer from lack of intelligence, know-how, experience, or even opportunity.

Leading is not about making them smarter but about recognizing their worth. One of the things I see quite often is that women don't tend to raise their hands and ask for the chance to step up, lead, and perform. They know they are more than capable, and yet time and time again, when presented with an opportunity, they don't step up and ask for the assignment. So we see that there is a gap between a woman's ability (competence) and showing up and raising her hand (confidence).

My ultimate goal for writing this book is to inspire women to find that click. I want to help the woman who possesses competency and proficiency in her work, someone who shows up and knows *how* to work, but who is simply not asking for the promotion that she deserves or raising her hand for a plum assignment that she knows she would crush if it came to her. And there doesn't even have to be a promotion or an assignment at stake. Women need to understand that they can start today, right where they are. They can speak up, they can be their own advocates, and they can recognize their own value and carry that into the next meeting, conversation, initiative, or project.

According to the research firm McKinsey & Company, 83 percent of women currently in middle management positions desire to move to the next level at work, while more than 50 percent say it's important for them to have a leadership role in the organization. So the gap between women and leadership isn't coming from them not being interested. Perhaps it could be that they are not letting people *know* they are interested.

For many women, this is the place where confidence could be getting them to the next level—and insecurity is keeping them back. Ellen East of Time Warner explains, "I really do think it's all about being comfortable. I think if you are comfortable with who you are and how you're presenting yourself to the world, then you will be confident."

So leveraging your personal skills is about recognizing that you are as capable—or even more capable—than the people around you. I read an article once that said that if a job is posted in an organization and there are 10 qualifications listed for getting it, a woman will read those 10 items and say, "Well, I don't have what they're asking for. I only have eight and so I am not going to apply for this job." Yet for the very same position, and those very same 10 qualifications, a man may say, "Well I only have three and I am totally going to get this job!"

Now, just doing the simple math here, if every woman who doubted herself over having just eight qualifications showed up anyway, one of them would most likely get the job over those confident guys who might have only three qualifications. Not every time, but certainly much of the time. But if you never show up, guess who's getting the job . . . every time?

In talking about the difference between how men show up at work versus how women show up, Vernice "FlyGirl" Armour, whom we met earlier in this book, points out, "Guys are more vocal about their 'stuff.' A woman may be confident in her job and what she's doing. She'll keep her head down and work and think, 'I'm working super hard. I'm going to get rewarded. They're going to promote me. They're going to see how hard I'm working.' And she's confident in what she's doing. But guys are just going to talk about it. You know, he's going to voice what he wants and will be confident in voicing that."

Obviously, there is a difference between how we think about our own abilities and how that affects us asking for additional assignments and opportunities. The shorthand that I have been using lately when I talk to our women at Half The Sky is that you have to "show up, speak up, stop apologizing, and start where you are."

At the end of the day, that's what confidence boils down to: believing that you have what it takes and having the grit to show it.

Leveraging What Makes You *You*

After all the time I have spent in and out of corporate America, working and coaching, consulting and speaking, I honestly don't think we can separate our personal and professional skills because, quite often, they tend to be the same. Whoever we are, whatever we're like, at home and with our friends, at a party or at a ballgame, we tend to bring all of those things with us to the workplace.

For example, if you are detail-oriented at home—very organized and thorough—then you are naturally going to be detail-oriented in the rest of your life as well. It may even be what got you hired in the first place, so why deny it? If you are relationship-centric at home—a people person who enjoys socializing and befriending and conversing and sharing—you are naturally going to bring those things to your organization.

I think we do ourselves a disservice when we really try to parse out one way at work and another way at home. The skills we have in each place translate to the other parts of our lives. Whenever I see someone "transform" who she is the minute she walks into work, it makes me wonder how effective she is at her job because, after all, who she is is often what makes her so effective in the first place.

Of course, you may use your skills differently at work, but they are very much the same skills. For instance, people who are creative are creative everywhere they go. They're idea people. They can't help themselves. If you're highly creative, you likely think of ways to solve problems, even when they aren't yours to solve. You think Oprah can bite her tongue with friends, acquaintances, strangers, guests, or coworkers if she's inspired to tell them something that will help them? Ideas are in her blood and have helped her achieve success.

Conversely, if you're more of a reflective or introverted person, you are going to bring those same qualities to your work role as well. Both relationship-centric skills and detail-oriented skills have value—perhaps not in the same role, but at least in some capacity. The same extroverted, relationship-centric skills that make one individual such a successful salesperson may wreak havoc in the accounting department, which tends to be populated by folks who are required to work in a more detail-oriented, reserved environment.

Be Yourself . . . with Guardrails

That said, it's important to, as I say, be yourself . . . but with guardrails. In other words, you're not in your living room. You're in your workplace, so you do have to temper your behavior and fit your environment. Your company is not your family. There are times when you are going to have to make decisions about adult behavior in your work environment. This can affect how you:

○ *Communicate concerns.* Are you going to voice every concern? Every time? And to whom? Are you going to rant and rave if you don't get your way? Or will you be mature and find a more appropriate, professional solution?

○ *Show up when the team is struggling.* Are you going to pitch in even when it's someone else's fault? Or are you going to say, "It's not my responsibility" and go home at 5:00 anyway? Will you show humility and grace? Or will you hog the spotlight?

○ *Express yourself in terms of disappointment.* Are you going to pout, fume, and blame others for your lack of progress? Are you going to go over your superior's head and try to garner favor with her superior? Or will you consider the fact that you may have fallen short—and then acquire the skills you need to avoid that shortcoming next time?

○ *Conduct yourself in social environments.* Are you going to let it all hang out? Be "one of the boys" and forgo all propriety? Or will you have fun but still be sensible?

○ *Share information.* Are you going to be careless with gossip and rumors? Are you going to act like you're in the high school halls, tattling on a "frenemy" or picking sides with the "cool kids"? Or will you remember that you're in the workplace and value the art of discretion?

When you're at a work-related function, you're not "off the clock." You are always making impressions at the organization. If you are a super social partier—the kind of person who has one too many glasses of wine at a client event, or too many beers at the work-sponsored softball game—it affects your brand. You're there to have fun, not to be a social-media poster child. I promise you, these days, one racy or inappropriate smartphone photo of you making a bad choice at a company party, and all the confidence and competence in the world won't help you recover.

Over the course of my career, I have seen many young women make the mistake of thinking that after-hours events, parties, and social interaction with people from work doesn't matter. It does. And, increasingly, so does what you post on your Facebook page or in your Twitter feed and other forms of social media. You may think, "It's my personal life and none of the company's business," but if you want to be looked at as a leader and someone who is going places in an organization, then you want to be aware of how you're showing up—even when you're not at the office.

If your brand is important to you (and it should be), you have to be very careful about the decisions you make and how much you "relax" in work-related social environments. The same eyes that watch you during board meetings or on conference calls are watching you at the employee picnic, cookout, after-work happy hour, ballgame, and convention after-party.

You must know that while alcohol is part of many work-related events, it is not your friend. I have had to release an HR executive, several senior managers, and far more rank-and-file employees than I cared to because they acted out at after-hours events to the point where it didn't just hurt their brand but could have affected the organization's brand as well.

When you are with work colleagues, your reputation is always on the clock. This includes what you say in a voicemail, in an email, or in a text message. Nothing is private anymore; you have to be very thoughtful about how you "show up" in person, online, and in electronic communications. If you have certain personal qualities that make you successful, they will probably help you be successful at work. But keep in mind that any muscle overused becomes a weakness.

Profile in Confidence:
Natalie Nixon, Ph.D., Principal, Figure 8 Thinking,
and Director of the Strategic Design MBA program
at Philadelphia University

I definitely believe in "fake it until you make it." I think it might come from my dance background and training, where a lot of the times you have to do that until you actually get the choreography or the movement, but there is definitely something to just jumping in, trying it, and having the experience, and people begin to respond to you in kind.

It's this nice feedback loop and cycle that helps you to believe that you are worthy, that you are supposed to be in the room, that you have something valid to say and to offer. I think every next major challenge I've taken on, I certainly didn't necessarily have 100 percent of the confidence.

But I had a little bit of a reference point in my past, because if I got through that, I've shown up here. I can get through the next phase of this. There's always a reservoir of other past experiences that I can tap into to help me get to the next level of 100 percent confidence.

I think sometimes you just need that little bit to go forward. When I was in my first year in college, I auditioned for the dance company at Vassar. I didn't make the company and I was crushed. I was just devastated and I moped around for a few days and just felt sad, and dejected, and rejected, and then it occurred to me. I thought, "Maybe I can serve as an understudy."

So I went to the dance professor, who was head of the company, and I pitched to him this idea. I said, "I don't know if you have understudies, but because I didn't get into the company would it be all right if I still was able to attend rehearsals and I served as an understudy?"

He said, "Well, we've never had anyone do something like that. Let me think about it."

And he talked it over with the other dance instructors and said, "Sure." He invited me to do that. By the second semester of my freshman year, I was admitted in to be part of the full company corps. And it taught me a huge lesson that you're not going to get picked for everything. And dance education certainly teaches you that.

The real value of your character is: How do you deal with adversity? How do you deal with rejection? How do you deal with being told no?

The Takeaway

That "click" I mentioned at the beginning of this chapter is the sweet spot where your competence and your confidence meet. They're not mutually exclusive, so you won't hear or feel the click if you just do one but not the other. So, for instance, if you are only leaning on the fact that "Gee, I am a great relationship builder" but you are not getting things done, or you are really high on execution but nobody in the organization knows who you are, then you're not clicking.

That's why my 4 Rs of Success are so effective in providing you with the tools you need to go from competence to confidence and then on to leadership. Only when you factor in relationships, reputation, results, *and* resilience will you get to the next leadership level. But take heart: We're halfway there!

8

Building Your Personal Brand

Your personal brand is a combination of all that we've discussed so far: reputation, gravitas, appearance, communication, presentation, fashion, style, humor, grace, grit . . . all the things that pervade and surround you as you go about your day. It is both a reflection of and extension of you. The more purposeful you are about how you present your brand, the more powerful it will be.

The Evolution of a Personal Brand

My own personal brand evolved gradually over the years. Naturally, when I first began my career, I wanted to please and serve and grow and learn, which didn't allow for as much branding as I might have liked. As I grew in experience and position, as I began to get the lay of the land at each subsequent company where I worked, I could refine and enhance my brand to both adapt to the organization and exert my influence over it.

Today I am seen as a risk taker, as powerful and confident, as someone who helps women become leaders and helps leaders become better leaders. I am seen as someone who is influential, who has the ability to turn an idea into an actual outcome. I am seen as someone who is willing to help others and to hold them—and myself—accountable.

That inspires people to engage me, because most people want problem solvers, not problem makers.

I am not an extrovert by nature. I have a lot of introverted qualities and I like to be by myself. But because I am a storyteller and because I enjoy being in front of groups of people, I have gradually become more comfortable being in front of others—so much so that I work as a public speaker. People are shocked when I tell them I don't love parties and always being with a group of people.

Naturally, I have learned a number of things over the years. I have learned to modify my brand, for instance, because some of my qualities have not served me well. I am someone who needs attention and likes to be in the center of things. That can alienate some people. They feel that I am just "taking over." Because I'm such a talker, I can be seen as someone who does not listen. It's important to understand that self-awareness of what makes you good at what you do is also the self-awareness that makes you question yourself by saying things such as:

O *"Hmmm, how do I make sure I am open to these other things?"*

○ *"I am listening to others more now."*

○ *"I do not have to be right all of the time."*

○ *"I may not feel like being social but networking is important to me."*

○ *"Am I letting others share their ideas?"*

Recently, I participated in an exercise with a group of 10 people whom I had just met. Only a few minutes into the meeting, the facilitator had everyone do a "first impression" exercise. Each of us was asked to select four of the people we had just met and talk about our first impression of them by responding to the following: "List three reasons why you would want to work with this person and three reasons why you might not want to work with this person. And . . . *go!*"

Seven of the other 10 participants decided to give me feedback. For starters, the positive things they listed when wanting to work with me were that they felt I was powerful, strong, direct, and professional. Interestingly, the negative things about me were the same things as on the positive list! I thought this example was a perfect way to describe the decisions we make about people so quickly and about how our brands get communicated even when we haven't had much time to communicate. As a marketing friend of mine says, "Even when you're not intentionally marketing, your brand is communicating." Think about it and you'll see that it is the same with your personal brand. People are ascribing qualities to you based on what they see when you show up.

"You can't take things personally," says Jill Campbell. "You have to learn from it and move on. It's really important to learn from feedback so you understand what went wrong or what you did that caused something to occur, but from then you gotta shake it off and move on. And I think that makes you stronger because you know not to do something the next time around. That goes back to being very self-aware."

You have a brand whether you manage it or not. Your brand and your reputation are interchangeable. How people see you and how they work with you, work for you, or even lead you are critically linked. There is an exercise I do in one of my workshops where I just start tossing out words like "lazy," "contradictive," and "negative." Then I ask the group, "Now, do any of your coworkers pop into your head when you hear those words?" Almost everyone immediately nods and smiles and says, "Yes."

Sadly, that is the brand of that person each workshop participant thought of. If that person were you, and enough people had begun to see you that way, your brand would have a direct impact on how effectively you did your job. And if your brand is negative enough, for long enough, it can seriously affect what happens in your career. That's why I want you to create a strong, powerful brand that's full of executive presence and courageous leadership!

Profile in Confidence:
Sophia A. Nelson, Esquire, Founder of Nelson Strategies and author of *The Woman Code*

To be honest, I've never not been confident a day in my life. I guess that makes me kind of lucky as women go. So I don't have a story to share where I've never been confident. But I've certainly had moments of fear, I've had moments of not thinking that I could get where I wanted to go. Not because I didn't think I was capable, but perhaps there were other obstacles or things that I needed that I couldn't get or didn't have.

I think it's so important for women to get the different layers of what makes us operate—and how we have to peel through those layers to get what we want.

The first way is to make sure you are surrounded by people who affirm you and speak positive things to and about who you are, what your gifts are, and how to manage them.

The second way that you build confidence is you love yourself, you respect yourself, you know your value, and it is obviously very linked to who you know—who's talking to you, what they're saying to you, what they're saying about you. So, your confidence levels are really dependent on how much you think about yourself.

If you'll look at Oprah Winfrey, Arianna Huffington, and Michelle Obama, these are women who overcame great obstacles. Oprah, for example, grew up very poor, she was raised by her grandmother, she'd been sexually abused, African American, not very attractive by her own admission, and overweight, right? So, if you look at Oprah, everything in Oprah's surroundings of life told her she would be unsuccessful. Black female at a time—you know, she's 60 years old, Oprah grew up in a civil rights era context.

So everything in Oprah's world would've told her she couldn't succeed. But Oprah has said many times that the reason she succeeded is because somewhere deep inside she knew she was destined to do something great with her life. She knew she was meant to be more than a maid, the help, or more than a schoolteacher, or more than a nurse, which would've been the only thing black women of her time could have been, but yet she still succeeded.

Michelle Obama grew up in a three-room house. South Side of Chicago, pretty poor, with her brother, mom, and her dad. And went to Princeton, went to Harvard, is now the First Lady of the United States. So, again, everything in her circumstances would've told her she was limited, but she had parents who pushed her, she had people in her community who saw something good in her, and so it absolutely propelled her to greatness.

Arianna Huffington, a Greek immigrant, marries a congressman, has two little girls, she's a stay-at-home congressman's wife, and her husband cheats on her, right? And it's public. You're humiliated by this. But Arianna Huffington turned that around, of course, and became a talking head. Then she starts *Huffington Post* and it gets bought by AOL. And, well, the rest is history; she's a billionaire.

And so, these three very different women, very different upbringings—in the South, the Midwest, and an immigrant to the United States—they end up being very successful women, because they knew who they were internally and so their confidence came from a place within. It didn't matter what other people said or how they tried to limit them.

Everything we need to win in life is really already inside of us, and that's really that little voice that says, "You can be an artist. You can be an author. You could be a journalist. You could be a doctor, a lawyer, an engineer. You could be the PTA president. You could start the Moms Against Drunk Driving organization." Whatever it is that women do, it's usually inside of us.

What Goes into Making a Brand?

You build your brand on two levels: One is consciously, the other unconsciously. You have control over both, but the unconscious brand building takes the most effort to manage. Case in point: I once worked with a woman who was negative every time I met her. She had a list of grievances and aired them at every available opportunity. There came a time when she could have been on my team, but I didn't even seriously entertain the idea because she sucked the oxygen out of the room. I'm sure you know people like that, and you would probably make that same decision.

Now, think about how other people see you. Are you the person who sucks the oxygen out of the room? Or are you the one who adds life, ingenuity, passion, and purpose to every meeting? And, what's more, is your personal brand communicating that every time you enter or exit a room?

I like to say that your brand is not always the product you deliver, but your delivery of the product. If you're a good marketer or an expert widget maker, but every time you interact with someone you do the "sigh of death"—you know, that long-winded sigh where your shoulders slump—it doesn't matter how good your product is. If your delivery makes customers or clients uncomfortable, they won't be coming back anytime soon.

No one wants to work with people who are constantly negative or, on the flip side, those who are positive and fun to be with but who just sit around and don't get things done. People may like you, but will they hire you? Promote you? Buy from you? Engage you? Remember, not competence *or* confidence, but competence *and* confidence. That's the "click" we want to find for your own personal brand.

One more way to look at your brand is to consider the kind of energy you put into it: Is your energy negative or positive? Are you a "glass half full" or "glass half empty" person? I'm not saying that you must be a "glass half full" type; we all have our natural inclinations. What I am saying is that you have to understand how your energy comes across. If you are always perceived as negative, it's going to impact your brand. It's also important to "filter" the water in your glass, so that you are being appropriate for the work environment. For the "glass half full" person, bad corporate news may be met with "Oh well, tomorrow's another day," when a more serious tone is expected, and vice versa. The good news, generally speaking, is that you can learn how to temper your natural inclinations and build on your executive presence so that your brand and your delivery are focused and effective.

Steps for Building a Strong Brand

In order to build a good brand for yourself, you first must define what "good" means to you. What, exactly, do you want to portray? Frankly, there is no right or wrong answer. I think everyone's definition of what makes a "good brand" is slightly different. It also depends on the organization. Some companies not only hire for a certain type of brand but also actively encourage it throughout the employment process.

So it becomes a delicate balance of how you want to show up and what it will take to be effective and, honestly, rewarded within the organization. Ultimately, you must be true to yourself and build a brand with which you can be comfortable. That said, here are some general rules for positive brand building:

O *Start from strength.* How you show up at the beginning matters. Make a good first impression and your brand will come built-in. Looking someone in the eye, having a firm handshake, and the confidence of how you are carrying yourself all help to create and communicate a strong brand. Conversely, the same holds true for when you make a poor impression. That can linger as well. Be attuned to how you show up. Take a moment to be composed, to quiet the fears, to know and feel you are accomplished.

O *Don't sacrifice your principles.* It is important that you lead with courage, conviction, and compassion. If you're in a position of authority in your career, this is not just important; it's imperative. And if you recall from Chapter 6, on courageous leadership, the person who can tell the truth, who has the courage of conviction that this is the right thing to do, and also has compassion for the team and the company is the one who will stand out and be looked at as a leader. Know what you stand for and be true to your principles.

O *Communicate effectively.* Think about this for a minute and you'll see that quite frankly, we teach others how to treat us. The more effectively you can communicate, the more subtly you "tell" people what your brand is without actually spelling it out for them. There are many subtleties in communication, nuances in nonverbal behaviors, in addition to word choices, that help to tell others what you mean and what you stand for.

O *Share and share alike.* Give as good as you get, and recognize that the quality of what you receive is based on how willing you are to give. Be seen as someone who shares information and, in return, others will share information with you. Follow up when you say you will. Don't overpromise and underdeliver. In fact, underpromise and overdeliver. People will be surprised and delighted!

O *Be flexible and keep practicing.* Be able to adapt and course-correct as needed in an organization. Strong leaders say "we" a lot more times than they say "I," but they are still capable of "I" statements when necessary and are willing to fix things. Ellen East confesses, "I am at the very highest level of management in my company, but there are still situations that make me nervous. As the chief spokesperson for a large Fortune 130 company, sometimes I'm asked to speak about things that I don't have all the information about, that I feel a little nervous about, that I haven't practiced an answer to, and I do get nervous. The only time I feel confident in that situation is when I've had a lot of time to prepare and practice. I think I've learned how to present myself in a way that makes me look like I am confident. I know that for me, it's all about preparation and practice."

O *Encourage others to succeed, and they will.* The best leaders want people to do well, and people instinctively know that—and believe that—about them. Leaders who support their teams, provide resources, and remove obstacles in their way tend to have great success. I have also seen executives who end up struggling because they got results from their employees through intimidation, threats, harassment, and fear. They may be well known for getting things done and they may be rewarded for execution, but those leaders who beat up and demoralize their staffs don't tend to have long careers. Typically, they leave the organization and find another job before they get fired. They can boast of having great numbers before leaving, but they are going to have to improve if they hope to stay in one place for more than a few months or a year.

Ultimately, your reputation is not just *what* you do, but *how* you do it. Achievements are great but . . . at what cost?

The Takeaway

Over a 35-year career, I have had an opportunity to see senior people do well and, in some cases, do poorly. I have seen too many intellectually arrogant individuals who think they are the smartest person in the room. Even though they are in a somewhat enviable position, their reputation in the organization begins to get damaged because people say, "You know, this person is going to make me look small and criticize me in front of others." As a result, they get shut out of the information and opportunities. Or, worse, their leadership—and their team—suffers because no one wants to work with them, let alone for them.

Many times I have had clients hire me to help them find out why their team isn't producing as well as it once did. Very often, it's not because the team isn't producing as well or isn't smart enough but because members are not willing to put in extra effort because of the way they are being treated.

It's hard to go to work for someone who has a reputation as a bully or dictator. I have worked with people who have said, "I would rather be unemployed than work for so and so," because their boss's reputation is so negative.

Naturally, the reverse is also true: I have personally had two leaders in the past who were so positive, nurturing, and effective that I would go work for them again in a heartbeat. They are very smart and they lead with qualities that I find I am most attracted to in terms of passion, collaboration, and strong leadership.

9

Reputation Management

It takes time to cultivate a positive reputation, but it's well worth the effort. When building your personal brand, be cautious, purposeful, and passionate. That's because it can be extremely challenging to "rewrite" your brand once folks have decided what it is for themselves. Fixing a tarnished reputation is far more challenging than simply creating a strong one from the beginning.

Your Brand Audit

I urge women to determine their brand by conducting a "brand audit." A brand audit looks at what your brand is communicating right now, today, by breaking down the various factors that go into it. Here are a few ways you can get information about your brand:

o *Observation*. Look around and observe how people respond to you, verbally or nonverbally. Pay closer attention to whether or not you're included in informal meetings and conversations. Do people value your opinion? How do they respond when you speak up?

o *Feedback*. Don't be shy. Ask for feedback from people you trust and value. Simply inform them that you are working on a brand exercise and ask if they would be willing to provide a few words describing you. Jill Campbell says, "What I recommend is that you get specific feedback. Ask them, 'How I can improve?' Or, 'How do I get it so my voice is still heard, and I'm assertive, and I don't come across as aggressive or attacking? Can you give me specific examples? Because I really want to improve that.' You gotta put it back on them and why they think that."

o *The "mini" 360-degree evaluation*. Not everyone is going to be in a position to receive a complete and thorough 360-degree performance evaluation. However, you can do what I call a "mini-360" by asking people you work with and people you know socially to evaluate you. Ask them to tell you what they think your brand is about, and why. Dig deeper: Ask probing questions and clarify their answers. Ask about what your "look" says—your hair and makeup, your style, and how you come across. Pay attention to the adjectives they use to describe you. Do they match what you're trying to project?

The brand audit is a critical factor in our future success, not just in leadership roles but in every interpersonal relationship as well. Who we are shows up in every environment we're in. In other words, reputation and brand matter across the board.

Damage Control

Feedback on your personal brand can often taste bittersweet. You may hear some positive feedback, such as "you really pay attention to the details" and "you're very punctual," mixed with some not-so-great feedback, such as "sometimes you can be contrary" or "people perceive you as too aggressive."

Take some time to process the information; breathe deep and then, if you think it's necessary, set about doing some damage control to repair your wounded reputation. You can start to shift toward a positive rebranding campaign only if you acknowledge that the brand is weak, damaged, or even "bad"—that you've done something to affect how people view you.

Taking ownership of that is important. At some point, you have to look around at the landscape, consider your brand audit objectively, and say, "I need to adapt my style because this doesn't serve me anymore."

At Half The Sky, we want our participants to understand their innate styles and where they need to adapt, perhaps to soften the rough edges or blunt those sharp corners. We believe that having that awareness—firm, fair, and objective—will serve you well.

For example, I was talking to a woman the other day—we'll call her Brooke—who has a very bright future ahead of her in the advertising world. Brooke has been relatively successful at a young age because she's a proven go-getter with a host of achievements under her belt. Interestingly enough, however, she has also been fired a couple of times in her short career.

When we talked about that, Brooke did not see the connection between being terminated and having a potentially damaged brand. She was so driven toward execution—toward getting things done—that she often unintentionally overstepped her boundaries with her boss and her clients. She needed to deal with their perception.

Managing Perception

Perception is a major part of personal branding. It's not enough for you simply to know what you want to express in a meeting or conference call; you also have to be cognizant of *how* your words land and the impact they make on your brand. What you're doing may be in the client's best interests, but if you come off as blunt, hurtful, or off-putting while you're "helping" that client, you might not be around to finish the job!

In Brooke's case, she unintentionally makes clients feel like they're being talked down to or as if their ideas aren't worthy of discussion. As a result, she has had clients take her off an account—more than once. And it's not just external; lately, she's getting internal flak from within her company as well.

The other factor at play here is that people who work for Brooke have complained about her as well. After getting some additional feedback, Brooke is recognizing that part of her problem is that she is too direct. She has a high standard for execution and getting things done. But nothing else matters to her. For Brooke, it would seem, the end justifies the means and, as a result, she has hurt some feelings and bruised some egos on her trailblazing path to success.

Now in her new role at a new organization, as a part of reframing her brand and how people perceive her, Brooke has begun to allow other voices into the conversation whenever possible. She has worked hard on the individual steps to pull back, to avoid her natural inclination to control and dominate, and to be generous and inclusive in the moment. Changing her leadership style has not been easy, but Brooke recognized that it was important to her career and her brand. She has even gone back to people who reported to her, and to her clients, to make amends for having unintentionally shown up in a way that didn't honor their feelings. In that sense, Brooke is owning her behavior, taking responsibility for it, and, most important, changing it to more accurately reflect who she is as an employee, a boss, and a person. When you take ownership of something, you take responsibility; you're not just paying lip service. Then, your behavior has to change—and it has to change consistently.

Consistency matters. People hear what you say, but they watch—and judge—what it is that you actually *do*. If the two don't mesh, then your brand and your performance suffer. If you say you're sorry for something but then you do the same thing again two weeks later, you break the trust you asked for in your apology and people won't believe you meant what you said. When we see this happen, we register it internally and tuck away our perceptions about the person.

The Takeaway

To successfully repair a damaged brand, you first have to acknowledge the past behavior that's gotten you into trouble, work hard to change how you relate to others, and, finally, sustain the change so that people know they can count on it.

PART THREE

Results

Done is better than perfect.
—Sheryl Sandberg,
COO of Facebook

Relationships and reputation can only get you so far. Eventually, line items must be delivered and you have to prove yourself as a consistent and trusted leader. Ultimately, success is not just about being confident, but being *competent* as well: At some point you will need to back up what you talk about (confidence) to ensure that you deliver results in a timely manner (competence).

Promises vs. Results

It's easy to make promises; it's much harder to deliver results. Yet people expect you to deliver. That's why execution is a key component in building your leadership brand.

A promise is not execution. A promise is telling someone you are going to do something, which in turn becomes an expectation. For example, a promise of "I will deliver the spread-sheets to you by 10:00 in the morning" creates an expectation that *something will happen.*

In this case, the expectation is of a particular product—spreadsheets. And by "product," I mean anything from a PowerPoint presentation to marking up a brochure for your next recruitment drive to making hotel reservations for your team to showing up at a meeting (and actually being "present") to reporting the data you've been collecting.

So, a product is part of the expectation you've created by making a promise—and the result is the actual delivery. People begin to judge us—and our brand—on whether or not we can deliver, not just once or twice but consistently. But of course, delivery is just the beginning.

People want things done well, on time, and on budget—the first time, every time. Delivering a product that is only half complete and full of mistakes makes trouble for everyone. It irritates the people who have to clean up after you and begins to erode your personal brand if it continues to happen, again and again.

It's not just meeting the deadline that proves your capacity to lead, but the quality you produce. So when delivering results, remember these simple tips to stay on task, on target, and on time—every time:

O *Speed is great, if delivering before your deadline means that the product is also delivered well.* Most leaders (and I tend to be one of them) would rather have the work done right *and* on time. If the request is impossible to meet, then it's critical to make sure you provide updates on timing. Nobody wants to find out at 11:59 that your noon deliverable won't make the deadline.

o *Learn to work together with your team to produce better and faster results.* Don't even try to do it all yourself. Determine each member's skill set and assign duties accordingly for better and faster results. When you manage people well, you position yourself as a leader. If you're a team member, fulfill your promise to deliver your piece of the project on time and support the team's overall progress.

o *Quality is just as important as quantity, maybe even more so.* People won't remember how much you did but how well you did it.

o *Learn to brand yourself as someone who can deliver quality results in a timely, consistent manner.* Learning to focus on quality first ensures that when you need a little more time to get those quality results, your leaders will understand.

o *Take ownership.* Don't pass the blame to others. As Comcast's Andrea Agnew says, "Whether it's good or whether it's bad, you learn . . . Trust and honesty are characteristics that prevail every time in any given situation and in any relationship, especially the more senior you get into an organization. The higher up you get into an organization and in your role, it's less about the technical ability, because you wouldn't have gotten there if you don't have the technical skill set. It's more about the chemistry, the trustworthiness, the likeability. I've been in meetings when we're making decisions, whether it's to hire someone, put someone on a rotational assignment, whatever. And one of the first questions that comes up is 'Are they good people?' And what they mean is 'Will they show up? Will they deliver? Are they trustworthy? Are they supportive?' You know, those are the kinds of things that come up." Clearly, taking ownership and accountability is critical to show what you are made of—as an employee, as a person, as a *leader*.

While delivering quality results may be the *what* you are achieving, another aspect of leadership many people overlook is *how* those results were achieved. Employers aren't just interested in what was delivered, or even when, but also if people are thinking thoroughly through the task that was given to them before presenting the finished product.

In other words:

O Are you being efficient with your time management?

O Are you ignoring the product until just before delivery, and then rushing things to get it done on time?

O Are you overpromising and underdelivering?

O Are you showing a progression of thought, maturity, and leadership?

O Are you delegating or merely taking every minor detail on yourself?

Ultimately, success isn't just about what or how the product is delivered, but a combination of both—and a host of other qualities it takes to really achieve it.

Profile in Confidence:
Lily Kelly-Radford, president, LEAP Leadership, Inc.

To me, confidence is a blend of being comfortable in your own skin, gravitas, and good communication skills. It's the ability for a person to communicate with others with ease and comfort, not only being comfortable with themselves, but actually putting other people at ease and helping them access their own confidence. It also involves being in touch with your own emotional intelligence, very good speaking skills, and intellectual horsepower.

I had to overcome my fear of having someone else's projection of my identity become my own. And I had a lot of that being a woman and also being a minority woman. So this notion of faking it, for me at that time, was more about not owning that and standing firm on what I did know and acknowledging the things that I should know rather than pretending to know things that I really didn't. It was almost repelling a negative perception.

There are other things women can do to build their confidence, one of which requires gaining the required hard skills. I really think you have to know your stuff, and know it cold. It's about staying current, staying well read, understanding your industry exceptionally well, as well as understanding the competitive forces and adjacent industries that can affect your industry. So you can't just know your specific space, but other industry sectors that can affect your space and the outcome of your industry.

Knowing the political nuances, such as who the players are in your company, is important as well. So is being real clear about your own emotional intelligence, which involves several components such as self-awareness, what you're good at, what you're not good at, where your feelings are, can you identify them, what triggers them, that sort of thing.

Finally, self-management, understanding yourself and being aware of others and other situations, so you've got social awareness, and then having social skills.

The Dangers of Overpromising and Underdelivering

We all want to do a good job and impress those we work with and for. It's human nature to leap at every request, say "yes" to everything that's being asked, and then, when reality hits, worry about whether we can actually deliver quality results on time. But in our rush to be "people pleasers," we can often end up doing more harm than good by overpromising and underdelivering.

Obviously, promising something and then not delivering sends clear signals about our current performance level as well as our leadership potential.

Perhaps because they feel they don't have the power to say "no," or because they believe there is a real opportunity to grow and learn, women in particular have a tendency to say "yes" to things and, as a result, overcommit themselves despite their busy schedules.

When you make promises you can't keep and fail to deliver a quality product on time, your reliability and accountability will be damaged. It's better to be honest and say you can't make the deadline than to leap at the chance and then, at the last minute, deliver something half-baked or downright shoddy.

Leaders don't just look at the results you deliver but how you approach the all-around job from start to finish. If you honestly feel you can't do something in the time allotted, or even at all, it's okay to say you're underresourced and need this, that, or the other to make it happen.

Your boss would rather see you be demonstrative about why you're saying "no" than simply be a "yes woman," agreeing to everything while only delivering mediocre or subpar results that affect the team, the organization, and your leadership brand. Sometimes we need to learn a certain skill or acquire various resources before completing a task. If we don't ask for what we need up front, or even halfway through when we finally realize we're going to come up short, how will we ever do our job completely?

Understanding your limitations is part of leadership. No leader possesses all the skills she needs to succeed but instead recognizes what she doesn't have and surrounds herself with a strong network of people who do possess them. When we don't know our limitations, we damage our brand by overpromising, underdelivering and, in general, being unreliable.

If you are somebody who is all talk and no show, offering plenty of smoke (promises, promises) but little or no fire (delivery), people will catch on quickly and it will damage your brand to the point where you're overlooked for additional responsibilities and opportunities.

Profile in Confidence:
Sara King, Principal, Optimum Insights, Inc., and leadership development thought leader

When I think about women who are confident, one thing that's noticeable right away is how a woman carries herself. You can tell when someone walks into the room if they're standing tall, taking command of their surroundings, that's something that's first noticeable. I find that individuals who are confident are really good at looking others in the eye and focusing on others.

This means they're confident—and comfortable—enough in their own skin that rather than needing to draw attention to themselves, they are good at focusing on other people. To me that's a real differentiator because someone who is really confident can walk into a room and command it, but they don't need to draw attention to themselves. So, someone who can walk into a room, meet people, look them in the eye, but begin to really be focused on the others and asking good questions about them, I find that a mark of confidence. A person who is confident also isn't afraid to share an opinion and to be fairly visible with her opinion, and isn't afraid of criticism.

Now, when I said someone who's confident isn't afraid to share an opinion, at the same time, I think they're willing to entertain other people's opinion and, perhaps, even change their viewpoint. We often focus on the notion of individuals when they don't have enough confidence, but I think that there is also a problem when someone is overconfident, and they have blind spots that, perhaps, trip them up—and are not willing to see it. So people who are overconfident may not admit that they're wrong, and may not be willing to shift an opinion, so I think that comes with its downside as well.

One of the pieces of advice I received early on in my career was about owning and developing an expertise. You know, we enter a part of the business, whether it is marketing or sales or finance or legal or human resources, and we develop some functional expertise. Then, as we grow our careers, the necessity to move away and be more of a generalist helps us continue to be a value to the organization. We really have to grow and diversify our experiences.

At the same time, I think continuing to own and develop an expertise says that you create even more value. You can continue to be a go-to person, but you've got to have a variety of experiences. So, it's really managing the dynamic between getting a variety of experiences, being a generalist, being a systemic and strategic thinker. At the same time, I really believe that having an expertise that you can continue to fall back on can build your confidence as well.

The Takeaway

When it comes to competence, delivering results is visible, physical proof that you can be relied on to do what you say you are going to, time and time again. Flash, sizzle, and hoopla are great, but leaders prefer hard, fast, deliverable, and measurable results to a flash in the pan.

Sure, everyone likes a "go-getter," that person who is always up for a challenge, positive about opportunities, and eager to please. But everyone *respects* a "doer," somebody who consistently and expertly achieves results on a consistent basis.

The more often you deliver quality results on a consistent basis, the more people will see you as someone who is reliable and the more opportunities you will be given as a result.

When you hear people say someone is "all sizzle, no steak," it means he's great at making presentations and smiling and playing the game, but bad at actually showing up with quality work that can be counted on consistently. Getting your work done and staying on task is enough to keep your job, but getting results and actually being proficient is what it takes to get you to that next level.

To deliver quality results every time, or even to deliver better results more often, think through the problem you are working on and see how you can deliver more. Connect the dots to take your work from good to better to best. Learn to be less tactical and more strategic. Use your team, resources, network, and delegation skills to get more quality work done in less time.

For instance, let's say you're working on a large project and you hear about a potential product or service that might have some synergy with what you're doing. Following up on this, being aware of the possibility that this find can add to the value of the project, having the time and resources in the project time-line to research this, and finally, bringing this to the attention of your boss can have lasting value for the company and for you as a leader. None of that would have been possible had you merely been phoning it in.

Part of connecting the dots is beginning to shift out of tactical thinking into strategic thinking. That's where people will begin to see you as someone who makes a real difference.

10

From Tactics to Strategy

Being tactical is a step in the right direction, but many women remain neutralized in the workplace by a decided lack of *strategy* linking their tactical strengths, even their personal accomplishments, with their more strategic, leader-centric thinking.

What Is Your Strategy for Success?

For many leaders, particularly those in the middle of their careers, being tactical is more about being "in the weeds" and executing on someone else's plan than it is about being on a path to bigger and better opportunities.

Most people spend their days in a tactical mindset, focusing on grinding out the day-to-day work that accumulates on their desk—clearing the "in-box" to the "out-box."

Great tacticians are obviously valuable. They get work done, consistently, on time, and with quality and skill. The challenge for many women leaders lies in being rewarded for their great tactics, and then getting pigeonholed as "just" great tacticians. That's a nice problem to have, but it's still a problem because then all such a woman will ever be is a tactician.

So you're a great project manager and your results are excellent in terms of delivering tactical components, but . . . what's next? The more you're rewarded for your tactical skills, the harder it can be for you to delegate. That's because the more tactical you are, the less strategic, especially about relying on other people to get things done. A tactical person tends to keep his head down and focus on his role, often to the exclusion of others. Strategic thinking, however, is less about producing results in isolation and more about how people, opportunities, and resources connect with one another to achieve results.

Don't get me wrong: Being tactical is good. The problem is whether you can evolve from a tactical expert into a strategic expert who can coordinate resources, people, and opportunities.

It's almost impossible to be strategic without at least some tactical ability, but then again, how you can ever hope to be strategic if you are always in the weeds doing everything yourself and never lifting your head up to see the bigger picture?

Clearly, the benefits of being tactical include the fact that you have the ability to complete a project from the beginning all the way to the end. That kind of skill becomes invaluable in an organization. After all, not everyone has that skill set, and not everyone is willing to do all the work herself. But where do you go from there? Where is "up" when you are the only one who can see a project through from inception to completion? And how can you ever move up when you're so good at getting things done that you never get a chance to do anything else, particularly on a higher, more strategic level?

We call having that kind of tactical ability *reaching a plateau*. You're producing results, but you aren't allowed to go any further because your expertise is just too valuable where you are. Being too valuable to promote may be flattering, but if leadership is your ultimate career goal, flattery won't get you a corner office.

The challenge of reaching such a plateau is that people in leadership don't see you as someone who can work on more than the one project that's currently in front of you. So even though you've built a strong brand, you may find that it's a barrier to promotion or greater responsibility because it's heavy on the tactical end of execution but light on strategic vision.

At Half The Sky we often see women who struggle with delegation because they are tied too closely to being tactical, as if that were the peak and not the plateau. Rather than let someone else take the ball, they have to hike it, run it, pass it, kick it, and score all by themselves.

Trust me, bosses want you to be good at delivering results, as well as mastering the tactics that lead to those results. But if that's all you do and you aren't able to transfer your skills into something more strategic, you might find it a struggle to get to the next level.

John Baldoni is the author of *Lead with Purpose: Giving Your Organization a Reason to Believe in Itself* (AMACOM, 2012). In an article for *CBS Money Watch* called "Getting the Strategic vs. Tactical Balance Right," Baldoni writes, "For many people, the transition from tactical to strategic decision-making is daunting . . . One thing senior leaders can have a hard time doing is learning to let go. In other words, they operate in their new job just as they have in their old job, and typically to poor effect. By contrast, good leaders learn to step back even when it means giving up what they enjoy doing."

The Takeaway

In a very real way, tactics lay the foundation for strategy. Learning to guide a project from inception to completion helps you understand its many moving pieces. But a strategic mindset will help you determine how best to delegate some of those pieces so you can put your leadership skills to work on other, more complicated and higher-level matters.

Strategy is high-level, forward thinking that shows you the next steps toward the project's growth, your own growth, and the organization's as well. It may help you to think of it this way: Tactical thinking is a short-term-gain scenario, where you complete a project only to be handed another project. Strategic thinking provides for more long-term gains as well as the insight into how this project could tie in with another project, how it relates to the future of your department, and its impact on the entire organization. Being able to step up to the strategic level means showing your boss and your team that you are capable of connecting the dots. Always understanding on a micro level what you are working on in the in-box every day and how it contributes to the bottom line of the business overall (the macro level) is a critical step to becoming a strategic leader.

11

Using Data to Your Advantage

Feelings are vital in forming your personal and professional brand, and even in fueling your burgeoning sense of confidence. But when it comes to delivering results, the use of data—i.e., cold, hard facts—is crucial in the all-important realms of decision making and, ultimately, influence.

I Second That Emotion

When we're beginning our careers or are new to an organization, conversations are less formal; risks are lower and outcomes less dependent on—and vital to—the organization's overarching success. For this reason, emotions, hunches, and instincts tend to play a bigger role in our decision-making process.

It's easier to sit around a room, informally, and make quick decisions based on gut feelings and work through problems on the fly. As we progress through our careers, however, risks are greater, rewards are on the line, and our decisions begin to impact the company in bigger—and better—ways. Gone are the days when you can just raise your hand and with little or no evidence say, "I think this is the right thing to do," and expect everyone to agree.

Naturally, your opinion is valid and it becomes increasingly valid the more experience and expertise you accumulate during your career. But at higher levels in a company, there is always an extra, added layer of assurance required to make decisions. People still want you to say, "I think this is a good idea and we should follow this through because . . . " However, the "because" can no longer be "because I feel like it."

Suddenly, your bosses, colleagues, and cochairs want you to tie those feelings to hard data that make everyone feel better about heading in that particular direction. Your feelings are good, but they are no longer quite *good enough*. Whatever the conversation you're having is about, the further you go in your career, the more you need to be able to back up your thinking with firm, measurable data.

Coming up in my career, I was not someone who typically used numbers, facts, and figures to support my ideas. I worked mostly on instinct and gut feelings to forge my early career path. But the more senior my roles, the more I was required to back up my hunches and estimates with cold, hard facts.

When I was running recruiting for a Fortune 50 company, I had to learn how to speak fluently in numbers and to begin interpreting data in ways that others could understand. For instance, what was the cost to the company—in dollars and cents, as well as in time and productivity—of every new hire and of every person we moved?

Although by this point I essentially "knew" those costs by heart and could sense, deep in my gut, the true cost of hiring, firing, moving, or promoting, learning how to share that knowledge through the use of facts and figures helped me prove my point and helped others see the wisdom of such decisions.

Not everyone has the same experiences and expertise as you. That's why translating your gut feelings into the language of business—a language everyone can understand—becomes more of a critical leadership skill the higher you climb.

Indeed, the more senior you become, the more costly your decisions—and the more challenging it can be to talk about those decisions without data to support you. After all, we're not talking about justifying a client lunch or filling out purchase orders for office supplies anymore. We're talking about the ROI of key projects, about influencing people. Arguing passionately about the resources you and your team need to meet objectives becomes more critical as you move up in an organization. Emotion is no longer enough to sway the opinions of decision makers.

We all tend to seek our own comfort levels. In my work, I've observed many women in senior roles, myself included, who feel more comfortable arguing emotionally rather than from a purely numbers point of view. They shy away from the metrics and don't want to talk about numbers *at all*, leaving them at a distinct disadvantage when everyone else comes prepared to do just that. Instinct and emotion are a vital part of how we do our jobs, but it's only one part.

As a result of their preference for instinct and emotion, some women tend to shy away from the metrics. They don't want to talk about numbers at all, leaving them at a distinct disadvantage when everyone else comes prepared to do just that.

Eventually, I learned that talking about metrics is a necessity. But even then, I didn't jettison my gut feelings or instincts; I simply made sure I was framing the conversation around metrics that supported my decision or request.

Once I learned to speak that language of cold, hard facts, I realized they were a valuable tool and not some indecipherable code I had to crack in order to do my job. In fact, learning to find the right numbers, decipher, interpret, and then manipulate them is a critical skill set that certainly helped me make a point faster and more effectively.

If I could go back and change something about my career, it would be to have learned that skill earlier so I could have been more confident and competent in it sooner. Not that I couldn't do it when I needed to, but it was like writing with my left hand instead of my right. I had just never developed that muscle. And I don't think I'm alone. Learning to find the "story in the numbers" and then using the data to influence outcomes is a powerful skill. And it's an area that more women need to pay attention to earlier in their careers.

Our instincts are what make us unique and, what's more, uniquely qualified to lead. Trust your gut instinct. But be able to back it up.

The Power of Emotions

We need facts, figures, and data to make tough decisions. But math is just math; anyone can learn it and use it to her advantage. Our instincts are what help us stand out from the crowd and, eventually, *lead* the crowd. Facts and figures help us support those instincts in a way that makes others see them as ironclad.

Instincts can help us predict future trends or even problems. I have had an extremely varied career because I listen to my gut instinct and have stepped up to preempt certain situations because my intuition told me there was a problem *before* something happened. No matter how good the data, facts and figures can't always do that.

Many years ago, I was sent to a remote retail location. The minute I walked in, I honestly and immediately felt that something was wrong. Everyone I met on the leadership team seemed overly friendly, but the store employees didn't look me in the eye. Everyone seemed pleasant enough, but my gut was sending up red flags every time someone I'd just met avoided eye contact.

As soon as I could, I went out into the parking lot and called my boss. "Something is wrong here," I told him. "You're going to want to send the audit team out." Sure enough, it turns out the person who was running the business had stolen close to $1 million from the company. He had been doing a lot of things that were illegal, actually, and many of the employees had been threatened that if they spoke to me about them, they would lose their jobs.

This was one example of when my instincts helped me on the spot, because I had no facts before arriving on site. Ultimately, of course, facts were what proved my theory that something was wrong, but if I had ignored my instinct, the fraud might have gone undetected for much longer.

You can't ignore your instincts, but effective leadership requires you to add multiple layers of data to support each and every theory. In fact, you have to reverse your way of communicating to lead with the data and follow with the emotions. You have to become someone who says, "Here is the data behind why we think this is a good idea."

For instance, you might be doing a marketing campaign and find that there's a gap between your messaging and the demographics of the group you're targeting in the marketplace. Perhaps you're targeting an audience that has become more urban, sophisticated, and multicultural than previously and the marketing language you've been using no longer speaks effectively to those consumers. You can feel the disconnect between your message and your market and even sense that the campaign isn't going to have the impact you want to achieve. But emotions alone won't be enough to get your team or your boss to shift the entire marketing message. You must have data to back up your theory; you have to connect the dots and present the rationale.

The more data you can provide that supports your theory (from national statistics, focus groups, Q&As, cited sources, traditional academic research, etc.), the stronger your emotional case as you layer on the facts.

I also think it's important to be somewhat conventional in the language of numbers. Don't make it so complex that no one but you can understand it, and don't take it to the degree that folks need to wade through dozens of graphs and charts to understand a key concept you could interpret simply in plain English.

Now, I'm not encouraging you to become a walking calculator who gets so bogged down by data you can no longer think for yourself, let alone trust your instincts. But I encourage you to get more familiar with using data and, beyond that, to understand the impact of your metrics on the business as a whole. This synergy between facts and instincts, and understanding how to harness both, can be an incredible asset as you progress professionally. Learning to speak the language of business and being able to hone your instincts are critical skills for advancing in your career.

Network for Success

Emotions are easier because they come from within, but facts and figures require a little more digging because you have to go outside yourself—and often outside your comfort level—to get them. Personally, I struggled in this area because I wasn't as confident in finance and accounting as I was in managing people and leading a team.

When I realized metrics were a missing part of my leadership portfolio, I quickly leaned on my network of professional resources to help me become more proficient. I learned that in every organization there are people in finance or accounting positions whose job is to help you help the company. I know that's a bit facetious, but at the heart of what these folks do is to provide the data that the company uses to make decisions to go forward by looking backward at last month's, last quarter's, or year-over-year numbers. Using these assets will not only assist you with learning the power of metrics, but they will provide you with the very facts and figures you'll need to support your instincts.

If you need metrics on a routine basis, building a relationship with someone in the finance or accounting department can be helpful. Developing that relationship and honing that skill can become a habit that secures your own bright future.

Make it an instinct—and a habit—to seek out facts *before* you make a presentation or request. And try to get to the point where you can bounce ideas off that finance or accounting person to see how she can assist. She too may have a hunch about what's happening in the numbers, and she can share that information with you—improving her own abilities in that area.

If you are fluent and strong in this area, try to help others develop their skills in this department by partnering with them on a project or two until they're fluent. This is a great opportunity to network with others, and it will help you grow as a leader and a valuable team member.

The Takeaway

Data is crucial to your ability to make informed decisions and "sell" those decisions to invested stakeholders. Such metrics can be intimidating, but once you learn to embrace the power data holds to influence others and support your theories, passions, and interests, it will be your ally rather than your enemy.

Remember, too, that data is not a substitute for leadership. Facts and figures provide the support you need to make the decisions your instinct has already told you are the right ones. Along with procuring and curating data, you must take accountability for the data and the decisions they support.

12

The Power of Accountability

Leaders must be accountable if they're to earn respect, and nothing provides that accountability like proven execution of projects that are steeped in quality and delivered on deadline. This chapter provides simple strategies for achieving quality results that improve upon your organizational role and build your workplace reputation.

Excellence Starts with Execution

Accountability starts with results. Without results, you have nothing to be accountable for and no way to prove your effectiveness as a current—or future—leader. Talk is cheap, but results are priceless. That's because results are a way to prove your potential and provide clear-cut, physical evidence of your excellence.

Execution—not just how fast you get over the finish line, but how well you complete the work—is the method for getting those results.

Companies are getting leaner and leaner, and most of us are getting asked to do more with less, a situation that often lends itself to rushing, incompetence, and the blame game. Don't fall into the "everybody else is doing shoddy work, so I can too" trap. Getting something across the finish line in a way other than what your customer asked for is not execution. Getting a spreadsheet turned in with bad data because you did not fact-check it—or even spell-check it—is *not* execution.

Excel beyond expectations by learning to execute effectively. Here's how:

○ *Manage your time.* The first step to getting over the "do more with less" hurdle is to manage your time more effectively. Often the "less" we're asked to do "more" with is just that: time. Learning to declutter your schedule, delegate effectively, and streamline your efforts gives you the time you need to execute with excellence.

○ *Manage your people.* This is where being less tactical and more strategic helps you achieve goals more efficiently and effectively. While managing your time, manage your people to ensure that their time is being used effectively.

○ *Manage your progress.* One of the simplest reasons we fall behind or get surprised is simply because the project has gotten away from us. To avoid this, continually measure and monitor where you are along the project continuum to adjust and reframe your timeline.

o *Manage your expectations.* As your deadline for delivery approaches, take your progress monitoring to the next level and manage your expectations accordingly. If you can meet your deadline with excellence, great. But if you discover you can't meet your deadline without sacrificing quality—or that delivery of the inferior product could affect the department's other teams or plans—step up, take responsibility, and either ask for an extension or more resources to deliver quality on time.

As you can see, if you expect your execution to support your leadership capabilities, you must achieve it within your current workload, bandwidth, and time frame. Ben Franklin wrote, "Failure to plan is planning to fail." Without planning accordingly, your execution will suffer. Successful execution means refusing to settle for subpar work—from yourself or your team.

Stand Up and Say Something

Accountability means owning the results—whatever those results may be. Most of us find accountability easy when things are going well or a project exceeds expectations, but true accountability is about taking ownership even when things go badly.

At its heart, accountability is about standing up and taking ownership. Good, bad, or ugly, the buck stops with you—and you alone. I find it extremely telling that most dictionary definitions of accountability use the word *responsibility*. Yet, most people don't want to look bad; as a result, they don't take accountability or responsibility for their actions.

Personally and professionally, standing up and taking ownership is important. Even if it hurts in the short term, it shows leadership. You can take responsibility not just for what you've done right but where you may have made mistakes.

Being accountable for your mistakes is an important part of leadership in business. Not only that, but it's an important part of being a leader in your personal life. It's too easy to ignore ethics nowadays by taking shortcuts and laying blame. But the fact is, careful eyes are always watching and good people like to work with other good people.

Throughout my career, I've learned that people forgive mistakes but they won't forget when you blamed those mistakes on someone else. Even if you're leading a team and the mistake was made by someone on your team, take accountability for the overall issue and own up to your responsibilities as team leader. Not only will it make the team better, but it will make you a better leader as well.

Profile in Confidence:
Natalye Paquin, Chief Executive Officer, Girl Scouts of Eastern Pennsylvania

There are a couple of things that we can do to help our girls build confidence. We can reward our girls a little differently, and push them a little more to self-select. Girls don't raise their hands after a particular age. They'll do it if you say, "Oh, Jennifer, you should try this. You'd be really good at it." Or "Meghan," or, you know, "Shauna, you'd be really good at it." And then when they do it, they knock it out of the park, but they don't self-select. So this plays itself out when girls and boys get in the workplace asking for money, right?

We praise our girls for good work, and we pay our boys for good work. So if little Susie is making up her bed and cleaning her room, we say, "Susie, that's so great. Your room looks so pretty." Now she feels happy about that praise.

Whereas Johnny who just raked the leaves, you don't just say, "Johnny, wow, the yard looks great." You say, "Hey, it looks great. Here's a quarter," or "Here's a dollar," or "Here's something." Or he'll say, "Hey, can I have X, and you give it to him. Girls usually, again, they don't self-select, so they don't ask for money because socially, we're not taught it is proper or polite. Whereas, the boys are totally fine with asking for compensation.

So then, what happens in the workplace is that women respond to positive feedback, because, "Hey, they said I was doing good. But they're not paying me, but, you know, they're giving me this positive feedback." Whereas, a guy, they don't care about positive feedback. It's like, "Yeah, that's fine. I have a family to take care of. And how am I going to get paid?" So, I would say that with girls and boys, we need to pay our girls and we need to praise our boys.

I had a goddaughter who, at 15, said she was going to keep an eye on somebody else's baby. And she was, like, "Oh, but this baby's so cute, I'll babysit for free." And I stopped her and said, "No, Arianna, you will not sit for free." And she's like, "But she's so cute. I really like her." I was, like, "No. That is work. You will decide, on an hourly basis, what is the value of your time. How much do you think you can make in an hour? And they're going to pay you for sitting for that cute little baby." Getting girls to self-select and paying them for doing something well is extremely important. Not just praising them for doing something well.

This helps us realize that it's okay to be compensated for doing something well. It doesn't feel bad, like, "Oh, should I take this $5?" Yeah, you should. You earned it.

The Takeaway

We all know what it's like when someone in a leadership position, or even a fellow team member, throws us under the bus. Don't be that leader or team member; don't be that *person*. Great leaders take ownership of their work as well as their team's, and they apologize for not meeting their deadlines, for not getting the numbers right, for falling short of the mark.

Saying you are sorry is an important part of accountability and being proactive about the problem, as well as minimizing any surprises for your bosses and customers as soon as possible.

13

The Politics
of Progress

Timing might not be everything when it comes to corporate leadership, but failing to read the signals of success has derailed many a career. We all have roles to play, and nothing shows hard work, dedication, loyalty, and commitment like helping your team achieve unprecedented goals.

Staying in your lane is important, but so is knowing when to move—up, around, or even outside the organization. This chapter discusses the politics of progress, one step at a time.

Follow the Road You're Traveling

At different times in our lives, we follow different roads. In high school, we're on one track; in college, we're on another. At our first job we're learning and growing as we go down one path, which won't necessarily be appropriate to follow after our first promotion.

The key to staying in your lane is to follow the road you're traveling until it leads somewhere else. In other words, it's important to stay where you are until it doesn't make sense to stay there anymore.

Depending on your company, your leadership, your industry, or your skill set(s), taking a different road may mean remaining in your current organization while taking a different position or transferring to another department or site. It may also mean leaving the organization altogether and finding the "fast lane" in some other company.

It's important to pull over and check the map from time to time, but if that's all you're doing, all day long—scoping out the next opportunity, looking for jobs, tightening your résumé, looking for the nearest "exit" or detour—you'll never be able to lead effectively where you are.

Leadership is a transferable skill. But if you can't lead at Company A because you're so busy trying to find an opening at Company B, you'll never be able to lead at Company B either, because you'll be so busy trying to finagle yourself into Company C.

The lane you're traveling in right now might not be ideal; it may be full of challenges, potholes, conflicts, and politics, but the way out of it is through it. Don't suddenly jump lanes and abandon the track before it's appropriate to do so.

Stay in Your Lane

Regardless of the career path you're on, there are times when you really do need to stay focused on the road in front of you and not get caught up in solving everyone else's problems.

Women in particular often slip into the familiar role of being the "fixer," the comforter, of constantly trying to help someone else regardless of our own needs. Not only is it in our nature—it's often part of our personality. But where does it end?

We all know "those people" who need our help—folks we are constantly rescuing, often from their own selves. We wind up doing their work as well as our own, which causes us to lose focus on the road ahead and remain stuck on the side of the road, waylaid by our "den mother" status on the team or in the department.

I'm not recommending you become a heartless, cold machine, but know your limitations and how much you can give to others before it becomes unreasonable. Staying in your lane is about being focused, resource savvy, and not taking on the burden of your peers who are not stepping up and doing their role.

I am formally giving you permission to keep your professional "blinders" on to a certain extent. Stop getting caught up in the drama of the naysayers or those who are constantly coming into your office and wanting you to solve all their problems. This is a business, and you have timelines and deliverables in your own lane.

At Half The Sky, when we talk to women about self-care, we absolutely encourage relationships and workplace friendships, but we stress that women try to avoid getting distracted at work and instead focus on the task at hand. You have to put on your own oxygen mask before you help others with theirs.

Sometimes staying in your lane is easier when you roll up the windows, crank up the music, and motor down the highway while focusing on the scenery rushing by and not worrying about where the other cars are going!

A Case Study in Dealing with Distractions

Dealing with distractions is never easy, particularly in today's modern, fast-paced corporate workplace. Meetings, memos, cubicles, open-door policies, departments, teams, projects . . . it all adds up to full days with frequent, numerous, distracting interactions. If we're not careful, those distractions can chip away at our daily performance and set us back, even throw us off of the path.

Case in point: I knew a woman—we'll call her April—who was very compassionate and caring at her workplace. April was the fixer, the den mother, the unofficial "ear" to everyone—and everyone's problems.

We all know someone like April, but do we ever stop to wonder why April is there, in her office, available to us at all times of the day or night? Is she there for our personal consultation, or is she just being nice while doing her work "around" her many visitors and their intrusions?

Well, there came a time when so much of April's attention was being given to those people who would come into her office just to complain and take up time, sometimes for up to an hour, that she simply wasn't able to get any of her own work done. April finally came to me, frustrated, and asked for help. In return, I asked her to tell me what was important to her. After thinking for a moment, April replied that her two children were most important.

So I told her to put a picture of her family on her desk. That way, when folks came in to ask her questions or ask for help with their problems, she could remember that she was working for her two kids. This would help her keep her focus, stay in her lane, and know where to invest her time and energies.

For a more practical answer, I told her she should just let these colleagues know she would love to talk and help them, but not at the moment because she was working. However, if they still needed her advice, they could set up a time to talk over lunch.

She was so relieved! These simple tips helped April tremendously and, as a result, she was able to stay in her lane and not get sidetracked by the colleagues who were constantly distracting her at work, pulling her focus away from what needed her attention. Two takeaways: First, if you are like April, know what's important to you and what you're working for. Second, figure out how to solve your problem (getting your work done while at work) but also be true to yourself (a compassionate and caring person who enjoys talking with others) and fair to your team and employer.

Politics, Progress, and You: How to Know When It's Time to Switch Lanes

Every organization is political, by its very nature. The corporate structure is such that everyone wants to be at the top, creating bottlenecks at various points along the way—from entry level, to management, middle management, higher management, leadership, and the C-level.

The key to using politics to your advantage lies in understanding the environment you are in and doing your own work while also maneuvering around this political climate. We call it taking the "political temperature" of an organization. What everyone (especially women) needs to understand is that every company has a political temperature.

When we ignore the political climate at work, we can often get blindsided, personally or professionally. Once upon a time in the cable industry, for example, my colleagues and I thought we were invulnerable to competition and/or global or economic threats. But look at the climate today. Getting too comfortable in our lane can close us off to opportunities that may arise as we travel.

Also, as our positions grow and evolve, there will be times when we need to leave, for our own good and the good of the company. I think we've all experienced that period in a job or career or company when we've essentially "quit but stayed." In other words, our heart is no longer in our work even as we sit at our desks every day.

It's important to pay attention to the climate at work in our own company and in our industries, and to think about, act, and react when it's time to finally shift lanes. To help you know when the time is most appropriate, pause periodically and ask yourself:

o Am I growing in this function?

o Am I learning anything new?

o Is there anywhere else for me to go?

o What's happening in the industry that I work in?

o Am I being fairly compensated?

o Am I experiencing creative and professional freedom at this job?

o Are my efforts being respected and rewarded?

Often, we are able to answer "yes" to most, if not all, of these questions. But the more "no" answers you give yourself, the more likely that your time to change lanes, and even companies, is closer at hand than you might have thought.

The Takeaway

It's important to pay attention to the road we are on and to ask ourselves questions. Would I have done a few things differently in my career? Certainly. Absolutely. Who wouldn't? But the reality is, I wouldn't know what I know today, or even be who I am, without all the roadblocks, detours, and, yes, dead ends I experienced along the way.

Sure, maybe I stayed at Company A a little too long, or left Company B a little too soon, but learning from those mistakes helped me at my next position, and the one after that. You always want to keep your eyes open for an opportunity that may be at the next off-ramp, but not to the exclusion of the good work you're doing in your current lane.

Stay the course, learn the road, complete the task, and, when it's time to change lanes, you'll know because you've learned from the exits you took too soon—or not soon enough.

PART FOUR

Resilience

*A woman is like a tea bag; you
never know how strong it is
until it's in hot water.*
—Eleanor Roosevelt

If success, leadership, and fulfillment are why you went into business in the first place, then understanding how you respond to challenges, disappointments, and crises is important. Resilience is the mark of all success stories, much as it is the mark of every good leader.

Many people think resilience is just about bouncing back from a challenging time or getting over disappointment or experiencing a loss in your professional or personal life. It is that, certainly, but resilience is so, so much more.

For me, resilience is at the very heart of leadership. It matters because it's about how people adapt and then are able to move forward. Some of us can get over a hump or a challenge or a loss, or even around an obstacle, but if we never process what we did to surmount that challenge and overcome it, we're just setting ourselves up for more—and more disastrous—challenges in the future. Resilience is about overcoming adversity and "winning," but—perhaps more important—it's also about adapting to avoid future challenges in the first place.

Jill Campbell says, "Resilience is really important. People whom I've seen succeed the most are the ones who get kicked in the teeth and get up quicker than anyone else. You know, they'll grieve, they'll feel sorry for themselves for 10 minutes, and then they just rally. I think they're fearless, but it's not a reckless fearlessness. It's more a willingness to take risks, step out there, make mistakes, but not see that as the end of the world. So resilience is really important, particularly in moving up the ladder in your career. And sometimes you just have to accept a 'no,' you know? That's the reality of how it works. You may have your heart set on something and it's just not going to happen and so you've got to know when to spend your time to get to 'yes' and when you just cut your losses [and move on]."

Triumphing over adversity is an admirable achievement, but if it doesn't become a transferable skill, or even a habit, it will never lead to true change, which after all is at the heart of resilience. The act of overcoming becomes a transformation. That is resilience.

For me, one of the hallmarks of resilience is how people learn from challenges, adversity, failures, even lack of opportunity. For instance, watch what happens when resilient people don't get picked for something or if they miss out on a raise or an opportunity or a promotion or a leadership challenge. For instance:

o Do they give up and blame others? *No.*

○ Do they storm out of their supervisor's office in the midst of a tantrum? *No.*

○ Do they go around bad-mouthing whoever they perceive "robbed" them of their opportunity? *No.*

○ Do they immediately go and vent on social media about the situation? *No.*

Sure, they may be hurt or disappointed or even jealous, but they don't let that stop the learning process. Instead, resilient people step back, assess the situation, do an internal "audit," and try to determine where they came up short. They ask:

○ *"Am I taking my job status too lightly?"*

○ *"Am I getting too comfortable in my role?"*

○ *"Have I been stuck in neutral too long and need to find another gear?"*

○ *"Is my paperwork getting sloppy?"*

We can all get into a rut in our work, but resilient people see disappointment, even failure, as an opportunity to shake the dust off, start anew, and reinvigorate their performance.

After her son Connor died in a boating accident when he was not wearing a life vest, Dana Gage founded the LV Project, which is dedicated to improving water safety and creating buoyancy in life. According to Dana, "You've got to be comfortable with discomfort. If you wait, you're never going to move forward with anything. You have to just keep walking forward. Don't be afraid of what might be across the bridge. What will happen will happen, so just accept that things are not always going to go well, and move forward anyway."

Throughout this book, I've asked you to do a few simple things to become *confident to the core*: Raise your hand more often. Get out there. Speak up. Stand out. And I realize that trying new things, particularly when you may not be used to them, often leads to disappointment.

So maybe you've been doing those things, speaking up, standing out, asking more . . . and it's just not going your way. You're not getting picked immediately; you may not be seeing direct results. Don't fret. Often, what you learn when you don't get picked is more important than what you may or may not learn when you *do* get picked.

Profile in Confidence:
Ellen East, Chief Communications Officer, Time Warner Cable

In the early days of my career, which I've been in now for 30+ years, I feel like I did have to fake it till I made it. I was often the only woman in the room, especially in my early management days.

I took my cues from the guys. I learned to take a seat at the table. I learned to speak up in meetings, but it wasn't something I was immediately comfortable with. I did have to push myself to do what I had to. I had to talk myself into doing it. I had to kind of gear myself up before a big meeting where I knew that I might be called on to speak up or make remarks. It wasn't something that came naturally to me.

So, I do think you have to fake it till you make it, and I think that's fine. I think practice is a way that women learn how to be confident. They build on their successes. So I think learning some of the outward appearance of what it looks like to be confident can build people's confidence anew, and then in turn make you feel more confident. And those successes just continue to build on each other until you actually are confident in what you're doing.

This is the story that I share when women ask me what I wish I had done differently earlier in my career. When I first became a member of the senior management team, I didn't quite understand that my job wasn't just to lead my function.

So I'd go into these senior management meetings and if an issue came up around the communications function, I would address it and be pretty confident, because that was what I knew. So I could speak about it confidently, and after my first year on that senior management team, my boss, who was the chief financial officer, took me aside and basically told me that I was failing out at the senior management level.

I was really shocked! I asked him why, and he said, "Because you aren't speaking up enough." And I said, "That's not true, I speak up all the time. I always talk about the communications issues, and when something comes up about communications, I'm always the first one, you know, to speak up about it, because that's my job."

And he said, "That's not your job. Your job is to help us manage the company, and to help us strategically figure out what we should be doing as a management team for the entire company. You only ever talk about communications. You don't participate in the other conversations and that's not what's expected of you now."

That was a huge "light bulb" moment for me in my career. I had to learn how to be confident, to talk about the other stuff and, for me, it was really digging in and learning about the finances of the company, the operations of the company, the human resources issues of the company, so that I could participate in those conversations, and feel confident that my contributions were adding value.

I do think, at least for me, it is about preparation and practice. I think feeling like you know your stuff makes you feel confident about it. I feel less confident when I'm put on the spot or asked to talk about something that I haven't thought about—that's my personality. Others who are better on their feet, quick thinkers, are able to do better without that kind of preparation and practice.

For me it has been preparation and practice that really helped, and I think that helps a lot of people. I do think it is practice. If there are particular situations in which you are not confident, taking baby steps to feel confident can help. I started out on panels where you have a couple of other people to help you in your answering questions. Then you move up to a presentation with a PowerPoint you know you can rely on, and then you're giving keynote speeches. You have to work your way there. Building confidence can be a step at a time.

And one further point to understand: No one escapes failure. Your boss or CEO knows that. Sometimes the failure is our own mistake, sometimes it's out of our hands, but if we can't be resilient in the face of failure, we can't lead others to success.

Suiting Up, Showing Up, and Falling Upward: How to Focus on Progress, Not Perfection

We all have things we dream about doing—a place we want to travel to, an experience we long for. For me, I wanted to skydive.

I'm not sure when the idea first struck me, but somewhere along the way, I wanted to be one of those people with the great skydive video and photos. One of the challenges about skydiving for me is that there is a weight limit of 250 pounds, which makes perfect sense. You're strapped to the body of a skydive instructor, and you're both relying on a little piece of cloth to get you to the ground safely.

For many years, I was never below that limit, so skydiving was just a dream. I didn't even talk about it to anyone. There are people who would have said, "Well, all you had to do was lose weight," which just didn't feel possible.

Then something clicked.

I found a way to work on my health and began to lose weight. The day before my birthday, I called a skydiving school in Las Vegas (where I had gone to celebrate my birthday) and asked to speak to the manager. I asked him about the weight limit and he confirmed it was 250 pounds. I remember telling him that he had better be positive, since I was going to come the next day to jump and if they told me I couldn't, someone was "going to get hurt!" He laughed at what I'm sure he thought was a joke. It wasn't.

I told several friends where I was going and then headed off to the skydiving school by myself. There was just something about this event that made me want to go alone and not have anyone else's opinion or voice in my head. There is a lesson in knowing when to hit the mute button on the crowd's opinion. I rode out to the school and found myself waiting to check in with a group of what appeared to be very hungover 20-somethings. I did not know that before you could fill out the application for the class, you had to be weighed on an industrial scale in front of all the instructors. It was horrifying, but it had to be done. I weighed in at 246. Having met my goal of getting under 250 pounds, I was sure the worst was behind me. But there was something else I hadn't bargained on.

In order to do a jump, you are required to watch a skydive instruction video about safety and the risks of jumping. All of that day's potential jumpers were asked to sit on a series of wooden benches. As the instructors watched us, we were told we had to hold our knees up to our chest for 30 seconds without holding our legs or without anything supporting our backs. The idea is to test if you will be able to lift your legs to assist in a standing/running landing.

Panicking now, I looked right and left, and everyone around me, including the hungover gang, seemed to be able to do this with no problem. I couldn't do it. I had lost more than 100 pounds, but I had no core strength. My legs started wobbling at about 10 seconds and that was that. The instructor who'd been assigned to me looked me in the eye and said, "That's it. You can't jump." Then he walked away. I sat there, embarrassed and feeling a sense of loss. Even though I had managed to get over the hurdle I thought would keep me from skydiving, another one had appeared unexpectedly.

How many times in life do we think we are all set, only to have a curveball come our way? Suddenly I felt myself worrying about what I would tell people when I got back to the hotel. What would I tell all those folks who were waiting to hear about my great adventure, only to learn that I'd only made it past the scales?

As I started to gather my things, the main instructor came over to me and sat down. He asked me if I was able to grab the front fabric of my pants and hold my legs up for 30 seconds. I reached down and grabbed the fabric on the thigh of my pants.

He looked at me and said, "Okay, I'm going to modify the jump for you." As I looked on hopefully, he explained, "All the other jumpers today are going to land in an upright/running style. I'm going to take you up myself and you and I will land differently." I finished the rest of the mandatory training, which included a video of a bearded lawyer who looked remarkably like a member of the band ZZ Top. Then they handed me a jumpsuit and I went to the locker room to change.

I came out of the locker room in my shiny silver jumpsuit, looking like a satellite dish, and headed to the waiting area with the other first-time jumpers. Now, if you have ever seen a skydive video, you have probably noticed how "wobbly" everyone looks. Faces are pulled back and everything is jiggly. When I got ready to head to the school that morning, I had "Spanxed" myself from ankle to bra. I wanted to be sure that nothing was flying out of place.

As my instructor started putting on my pack, he said, "Wow, you are very firm!" Hey, you've got to love the miracle of Spanx—my version of elastic courage. This was yet another example of "suiting up and showing up."

The jump was fantastic! Sure, the first few moments are loud and scary—the noise when you leave the plane at 3,000-plus feet and the sound of the plane and the wind rushing by as you free fall. By the way, you don't actually jump from the plane. You sit with your feet at the open edge of the doorway and dangle them there for a moment like a little kid in a chair that is too big. And then your instructor—who is strapped to you—pushes you out the door. It's one of those situations in life where there is simply no going back.

Once the chute opened, it completely transformed the experience. Suddenly, there was complete silence and I was able to look around and see the beauty of the world around me. I felt grateful for the opportunity to do something I hadn't always been sure I could ever do. As we got closer to the time for landing, my instructor spoke in my ear, telling me it was time to grab the legs of my jumpsuit. I could see some of the other jumpers from my group, and as they approached the ground, they were all landing in a standing/running position. Their chutes were trailing behind them. It was very cool to watch.

As we approached our landing, I held my legs and my instructor told me to lift as high as I could. Then we landed on our butts. That's right, I landed on my backside and we slid along the gravel and rocks for a few moments. It wasn't the most graceful landing, but here's the thing: I jumped and I landed. It wasn't as cool looking as some of the folks I'd jumped with, but the outcome was the same: I skydived!

Profile in Confidence:
Vernice "FlyGirl" Armour, Chief Breakthrough Officer, VAI Consulting and Training, LLC (first female African-American combat pilot in the United States Armed Forces)

What confidence looks like to me is when you show up, you're not afraid to be yourself. Or, if there are some barriers or struggles, you move forward anyway. That, to me, feels like the simplest definition, which borderlines on courage. You can't have courage without fear, but confidence is an inner knowing. Know that what you have, who you are brings value.

Let me speak from my personal experiences: We've all heard the analogy about falling off the horse and getting back on. I grew up on horses and it could happen where I fell off or got bucked off. You might seem a little shaky at first, but I think when your confidence is shaken, it's important to assess what happened so it's less likely to happen the next time.

It doesn't mean it won't ever happen again, but how can we lower the chances of it happening again? And, if it's something we really want, are we willing to go through it or risk it happening again because we know that we have to move through the failure to get to the success? Your confidence doesn't have to be shaken.

The Takeaway

All too often, we don't try something because we don't think we can do it perfectly and we won't look as good as everyone else. This is a great time to remember to focus on progress, not perfection. When I went skydiving, my internal story was not obvious to everyone around me. I could have easily missed an amazing life experience if I was too worried about how I wasn't going to do it like everyone else. But I jumped and I landed and that's all that matters. I trusted myself, I trusted my instructor, and I was willing to do what it took to make it work.

14

Being a
Change Agent

We often feel like we have to wait for change to happen, but true leaders act as *change agents*, forcing change upon a situation, team, or workplace when it's needed the most. Change agents are important because they make things happen in an organization, often as powerful and influential leaders. As we will see in this chapter, they can do this by forcing change, "editing" change, or contributing to it.

How Do You Deal with Change?

Not everyone responds to change in the same way. In fact, in your evolution as a leader, you have probably noticed a variety of types of people in the organizations where you've worked.

There are people who:

o Only like change they have created

o Like to "put glitter on something" by just tweaking and adding ideas

o Resist change unless it has value they can see, touch, and feel

It's important to remember that those different types of people *all* work in the same company, often on the same team. They won't react to change the same way as you do, or even the same way other team members and employees do. The truth is, organizations are changing—evolving, growing, adapting—all the time. So understanding how you deal with change is important.

Case in point: Recently, I worked with a leadership team. When we administered the Birkman assessment to identify passions, behaviors, motivation, and interests, 80 percent of the team showed a significant amount of stress around the topic of change. When we pressed them to explain why, it turned out that most of them didn't like change because they felt as if they didn't have a say in the matter.

Not only did members of this group want to know why something was happening, but they wanted to have a voice in how something happened as well. In other words, they wanted to be included in the discussion and have a say in how, even why, the change was achieved.

Discussions around how you feel about change are important because you can't be successful as a change agent if you don't recognize how you feel about change in the first place.

How Do You Feel About Change?

Let's stop for a minute and focus on you. How do you feel about change? Answer a few simple questions to understand your feelings about change a little better:

o *How does change make you feel?* When the idea of change arises, do you get uncomfortable . . . or optimistic? The only appropriate way to respond to change is to embrace it, but first you must understand how it makes you feel to ensure that you can respond appropriately.

o *Do you prefer to force change, or be along for the ride?* Some people like to be the change instigator while others prefer to be the change "editor." By that, I mean that they excel at taking someone else's idea and applying their personal strengths, skill set, and expertise to making it even better.

o *Do you like to brainstorm about change alone, or in a group?* Some people are more comfortable working in a vacuum as often as they can. Others excel in a group atmosphere where they can bounce ideas off one another.

o *Do you fear change?* Finally, many of us shrink from change because we know it's going to upset our personal and professional applecart.

Knowing how *you* react to change will help you be clear, focused, and empathetic as you begin to recognize that other groups of people have different needs—and you begin to address what those needs are when it comes to change.

The Takeaway

Change is vital for success, not only your success as a current or future leader, but the success of your team, your department, and, ultimately, your entire organization as well. To be a change agent, you must recognize both the power and pace of change. It doesn't happen overnight, nor do people always respond well to change. Jennifer Dieas suggests, "Be patient. Patience, patience, patience, and take your time and know your stuff. And then if you know your stuff, know you deserve a seat at that table."

Understanding the power of change and learning to be comfortable with it helps "brand" you as a change agent, something every company needs in these sophisticated, complicated times.

Why does this matter so much? Simple: Leaders want to see that you are on board to go to the next level. Being a change agent is about connecting the dots for other people as well as yourself.

15

Competence, Confidence, and the Emotional Quotient

Confidence gives us strength when challenges arise, and honing our emotional quotient, or EQ, is an absolute must for weathering the inevitable storms that arise on our career paths.

IQ vs. EQ: Is There a Difference?

So, what's the difference between our EQ and our intelligence quotient, or IQ?

INTELLIGENCE QUOTIENT

Your IQ defines your ability to process information. For instance, do you pay attention to details? Are you appropriately processing the data points you're receiving? And what is your cognitive ability between what you hear and how you execute on different projects or assignments?

Ultimately, IQ describes your ability to learn, calculate, process, and apply meaning and skill. Many people have a degree of both IQ and EQ, but we are more comfortable with recognizing IQ. This is probably because IQ is easier to measure. If you take a test, we can see your grade. If you're given a task, we can see whether or not you completed it. If we assign a comprehension question, we can see whether your answers are right or not. It's harder to measure your EQ.

EMOTIONAL QUOTIENT

As the term implies, our emotional quotient is the ability to understand the emotions we feel and to manage those emotions to work better with the team. As one might imagine, it's important to be smart (high IQ) but just as important to be in control of our emotions (high EQ) to have the optimum confidence in our leadership potential when dealing with others.

Many people lean heavily toward investing in their IQ while completely ignoring their EQ. Again, this might be because it's easier to measure and reward IQ. We are often taught, as women and future leaders, to be the "smartest person in the room." But no one ever says anything about being the most emotionally intelligent person in the room.

You can have a very high IQ and not have any EQ at all, which is a problem since EQ is vital for understanding human relationships and "playing well with others." We have to understand that we can be the smartest person in the room, but if we don't have any EQ once we actually get *into* the room, we might not be able to understand what is happening around us because of the way we respond to other people, the way they respond to us, and the way we all respond to what's happening.

Leadership Hangs in the Balance: The Delicate Dance Between IQ and EQ

I've talked before about the delicate balance between confidence and competence, and here again there is a need for balance when it comes to IQ and EQ. It's not just a matter of having one or the other, but having both in a proper balance to both process information and to manage our emotions and how we deal with others in a corporate culture.

Everyone has some level of IQ. It represents our ability to learn and move through the complex input of data and concepts that we must process on a daily basis. If we didn't, we wouldn't have a job in the first place.

EQ comes more naturally to some people than others, giving them a higher EQ than their emotionally challenged counterparts. People with a high EQ are usually seen as more sensitive. They can look at a situation, even one that's highly complex, volatile, or emotionally charged, and express their feelings clearly. They are able to express emotions and vulnerability and be more approachable to people who need a calm and rational response versus flying off the handle and overreacting. High EQ people tend to "bounce" a little faster, and better, than those with low—or no—EQ.

But not everyone possesses the maturity and emotional complexity that comes from EQ. It's almost like people with a low EQ don't see the signal from third base. They miss vital and natural cues that most of us notice on a daily basis. People with a low EQ are seen as having no—or little—empathy, understanding, or compassion. Facts, data, and processing—the hallmarks of IQ—are far more valuable to them than the emotions, understanding, and compassion possessed by people with a high EQ.

These are people who absolutely do not see the value in emotion, particularly in the workplace where it should be business as usual despite whatever outer or inner forces are at play. A merger, a buyout, a promotion, a success, a failure, a Monday, a Friday, or a holiday are mere data points for them to consider, while all around them the rest of the office may be celebrating—or crying.

But low-EQ people aren't wired that way. What I find really interesting about them is that while they are often seen as uncaring by just about everyone around them, this "brand" would actually surprise them. Their intention is not to be cold, distant, or removed, but that's exactly how they come across because they don't process emotions the same way most of us do.

The EQ Leader

So what do you do if this is you? How do you get a higher EQ if you've been so focused on IQ that you've basically ignored your own emotions and those around you?

Obviously, it's difficult to be a good leader. We have to juggle so many things—confidence and competence, quality and quantity, and now, our intelligence and emotions.

If you have a low EQ or simply want to refine a middling EQ, it's important to develop more self-awareness around your own lack of emotions and how others relate to you in the workplace.

Having a high IQ and processing data is a critical skill set that shouldn't be thrown out with the bathwater, so to speak. However, in this day and age when diversity, complexity, and emotional sophistication rule, you are going to be the smartest person in an empty room if you can't learn to appreciate, and lead, folks who may respond to emotions very differently than you do.

Here's an example: Years ago there was a woman—we'll call her Lisa—who was very good at her job. Lisa had a hard time having children. Success in her job was important to Lisa, but so was being a mother, something that kept eluding her. She was finally able to adopt a little girl from South America, and it was the happiest day in Lisa's life.

Lisa took some time off to help her adopted daughter adapt to life in the United States, and when she came back to work she was very happy about the balance in her life. She arrived at her office to find it full of balloons and greeting cards and confetti as her coworkers wanted to share in and acknowledge this wonderful moment in her life.

Her boss at the time—we'll call her Ellen—was a very high-IQ/low-EQ leader. Moments after Lisa arrived at work and began settling in to read the greeting cards and catch up on emails, Ellen had to walk through literally a sea of confetti to enter her office. Completely ignoring the balloons and cards and flowers and confetti, Ellen announced, "Hey, I need this report in 10 minutes" and walked right back out.

The moment was seared into Lisa's brain. While she dutifully complied with Ellen that day and moved forward, it was like a switch had been flipped off inside her brain. The impression Ellen made that day remained strong and influential as time went on.

Lisa committed herself to moving forward and always producing for Ellen—but not an ounce more than what was expected of her. She was efficient, competent, and responsive, but out of duty rather than respect. Lisa wanted to invest in her career but not in her boss-employee relationship, and it left Ellen at a distinct disadvantage when she occasionally needed Lisa to go "above and beyond."

Since Ellen hadn't even bothered to acknowledge the personal aspect of their workplace relationship, something that wouldn't have taken more than 10 seconds to do at the time, the experience left Lisa with a bad taste in her mouth. She performed exactly at the level of what she needed to do to meet her work demands for Ellen, but she would not give an ounce of effort more.

The Takeaway

Don't lean too heavily on IQ *or* EQ. Instead, find the right balance that works for you. EQ may not come as naturally to you as it does to others, but that doesn't mean it's not as vital a tool as a high IQ.

Instead, recognize that a leader with a high IQ and a high EQ always gets more from her people. EQ might not be important to you, or even your boss, but trust me—it's vital to your people. Ellen may have been a good boss, but she was no leader. If we can't lead, it will affect the bottom line because productivity is always affected by how we lead.

We've all had those bosses we go the extra mile for. They might not be perfect, but they inspire in us a desire to please them. Any time you see those people who can go the extra mile for the boss, I can guarantee you that boss has a high EQ and uses it to lead, bond, and communicate.

People don't leave their lives at the office door. They show up to the workplace with all kinds of challenges that are going on in their lives—their kids may be sick, they may be having financial problems, or any number of personal difficulties. As a leader, for better or worse, people are going to come to you with their problems.

It's not your job to be a personal savior, buddy, friend, or even counselor. However, you can't ignore what your people are going through and still expect to lead them. Knowing how to recognize emotions in others and handle your own will give you a higher EQ and higher productivity from folks who will always want to go the extra mile for you.

16

Learning to Bounce

When we are rigid, unyielding, and stiff, we break; when we are flexible, mature, and open to change, we bounce. Vernice "FlyGirl" Armour, America's first African-American female combat pilot whom we met earlier in the book, explains "the bounce" this way: "I think an important piece when your confidence is shaken is to assess what happened. What happened and how do you fix it, so it's less likely to happen the next time. It doesn't mean it won't ever happen again, but how can we lower the chances of it happening again? And if it's something we really want, are we willing to go through it or risk it happening again because we know that we have to move through the failure to get to the success?"

In this chapter, I reveal the secrets of growing your confidence, one "bounce" at a time.

Stop, Drop, and Roll: Putting Out Fires at Work and in Life

When I was a little girl, we used to see Smokey Bear teaching fire safety on posters and on television. Our teachers—and sometimes visiting firefighters—would teach us how to survive a fire by learning how to "stop, drop, and roll." It's a simple, effective message. So is learning to "bounce."

Bouncing is how you respond to difficult challenges in your life or work, and as one might imagine, it's a critical tool in learning to be more resilient on and off the job. So, what does this have to do with teachers, firefighters, or even fire?

Well, one of the ways in which I teach people to bounce is to use the same "stop, drop, and roll" analogy to address the little brushfires that inevitably ignite in all of our lives.

From time to time, we all wind up in a circumstance or predicament where we are embarrassed, upset, anxious, disappointed, angry—perhaps even crying. In such an emotional state, when we're so upset, we sometimes express ourselves through anger or frustration. Subsequently, we're not coming off as our best selves.

I call it "getting on the crazy train." Everything you do in that moment is directly impacted by the ride. It's not unlike an out-of-control wildfire, apt to destroy a lot of the goodwill we have in the organization if we don't extinguish it quickly!

STOP

The very best thing you can do at that moment is to stop running around and simply start . . . *breathing*. Assess the situation, look around, and see where the exits are; or, if possible, see how you can put out the fire yourself. When we're in a crisis that requires a bounce to be overcome, we have to be able to gather our resources so we can make clear decisions and provide a sincere action plan to achieve results.

When you run during an actual fire, the air you're displacing feeds the flame. The same holds true in life: If you panic, react, lash out, quit, or blow up, you only make the situation worse.

DROP

So, when you do this in life, first you have to stop and then you have to "drop" your fear. Your fear doesn't control you; you control your fear. I know it often seems quite the opposite, but the fact is your fear is 100 percent reliant on you feeding it. The more afraid you are, the more you feed the anxiety, pressure, and fear that made you afraid in the first place. As you begin to feel more and more fear, you begin to experience more and more self-doubt.

The fear and negative self-talk is so overwhelming for many of us that we often feel like it is an impossible situation, and whatever negative story you are telling yourself—"I'm such a loser," "This is all my fault," "This always happens to me," "I'm not cut out to lead"—only gets amplified.

ROLL

You have to stop feeding the fire. And the only way to do that is by rolling through the bad patch and off the crazy train. Tell yourself that this is a place in the road but not the end of the road.

Personally, I have what I call a "Hell No" button. It gets pushed when I make a decision that this is not how the story will end. I have had challenges in my life. One of them was my first marriage. It was bad for a variety of reasons, and I didn't handle it well.

I gained weight, acted impulsively, and my finances took a turn for the worse. I was ashamed and embarrassed. I was stuck. I knew I'd made a bad mistake in marrying this man. Eventually, it got so bad and I was so miserable on the inside that it began to affect the outside. I looked—and felt—*bad*. I just didn't know what to do. Finally, someone said to me, "Anything money can fix is not a big deal."

At the time, I was flat broke.

My fear kept me stuck. I didn't know what to do or where to turn. Then I realized I didn't need to go *somewhere*—I needed to go to *someone*. When I was willing to say to somebody that I didn't know what to do anymore, I finally got the help that I needed.

If I hadn't reached out to someone in my most desperate time of need, I'm not sure I'd be writing this book right now. Maybe that's why when I speak to women and, in particular, women leaders, I drive home the concept of "using your resources" so hard.

Back to my first marriage: I pushed my "Hell No" button and said, "This is not the way my life is going to be." I told my husband I was going on a business trip, and I never went back. It was hard, and I left with nothing but the clothes on my back and the skills I'd acquired in life, but it was my only choice at the time.

That meant that I had to rebuild my life from scratch, including my financial life. At the time, I had more than $60,000 in debt that my ex-husband had racked up, and I couldn't rely on him to clean up the mess he had made. I had to take care of it and, eventually, I paid it off. It was one day at a time. From the outside, no one had any idea all this was going on, but on the inside, every day was a struggle to get off my own "crazy train" and back to a sane, rational, livable life. I think back about how long I stayed in a bad situation and tell people if you have to do something to protect yourself, then do it.

Profile in Confidence:
Dana Gage, Founder, the LV Project

I watched a documentary on Theodore Roosevelt recently. In the late 1800s, Roosevelt lost his mother and his wife on the same day. Before that he was gregarious and full of life and determined, and after that he was completely broken. At the time, he said, basically, "The light in my life is gone."

He eventually pulled himself back through. And later he said, "There were all kinds of things of which I was afraid at first, but by acting as if I was not afraid, I gradually ceased to be afraid. Most men can have the same experience if they choose."

I think he was a real example of muscle and grit. He had the worst possible experience, and he pulled himself out of it. And for me personally, absolutely I think we've all been in situations where we have to create value simply by going beyond ourselves, looking beyond where we are right now. We basically look toward the destination, and that's how we get there.

If I had to sum it up, confidence is knowing who you are, not being concerned with who others think you are. Confidence is, "I know who I am and I'm not concerned with who you think I am."

There's a time in everybody's life when it's victim/Viking time. In other words, are you going to be a victim the rest of your life, or are you going to be a Viking? A friend of mine said that to me, and I think when we use the setbacks in our lives as an opportunity to move forward and not get stuck, that's what it's all about.

Something that I fear the most, I can learn from that. Case in point: Grasshoppers will often slightly rotate before they leap. They'll take a couple steps left or a couple steps right, and that's because they only can leap forward, so they have to align themselves first.

Align and leap! And that is so true: Get lined up, and then take the leap. And for me, that was just like a symbol of trusting my instincts, pointing toward the right source, and being unafraid to take the big leap. That's how you get confident.

The Takeaway

When we learn to stop, drop, and roll, it allows us to bounce back from any situation, personally or professionally. One way to bounce back is to tell yourself you can, and we do that by looking back on the successes in our life and counting all the triumphs we've made when we thought we might fail—or even when others told us we would fail.

I can look back on my life and see the challenges I have overcome, and that gives me the confidence to do more good things in the future. Bouncing back isn't about forgetting the past; it's about altering your perception of failure to perceive success. It's about replacing that negative self-talk with the positive reality of whatever situation you overcame and recognizing that if you did it once, you can do it again.

Resilience is transferable. That means if you've succeeded in the past, you'll succeed again. No matter how bleak the landscape looks at the moment, no matter how hot the fire burns at the moment, bouncing is the art of knowing that this is not how your story ends. There is another "happily ever after" right around the corner, if only you'll stop, drop, and roll away from the present and bounce toward a brighter future.

Failing at a project, having bad bosses, not analyzing the data properly, being inexperienced or naive, not assessing the workplace politics . . . you can learn from every single bad thing that has happened to you, and that becomes the platform from which you learn and move on to the next level.

17

The Importance of Stamina

The difference between managing and leading is much like the difference between a job and a career. The longer the haul, the higher the stakes, and the more you have invested in a role, a company, or a division, the more stamina you'll need for your journey from competence to confidence.

The Benefits of Stamina

You want to be in this for the long haul and not burn out. That requires stamina. We may get excited about an opportunity and then burn the candle at both ends, but fail to keep the pace when we finally land the job, position, or career we worked so hard to attain. Good leaders don't burn themselves out. Instead, they pace themselves to ensure that they learn effective leadership habits that will last their entire careers.

And it's not just at work. As women, in particular, we need to take care of our bodies, minds, and souls to achieve that work-life balance where we're not just sitting at our desks for 12 hours a day and ignoring our needs for physical fitness, good nutrition, and self-care.

I have tremendous personal energy and a joy of life. But as I've already said, I have had issues with my weight for most of my life. I work hard to be active because I know that the more active I am, the better I perform across all areas of my life.

Effective leaders know the value of protecting their health on and off the job. In fact, according to an article called "6 Daily Habits of the World's Most Successful CEOs" on BusinessInsider.com, "Regular exercise is almost as common among successful CEOs as getting up early. In fact, this is one of the first things that many of these professionals incorporate in the day. Andrea Jung, the former CEO of Avon Products, always got up at 5:00 a.m. to use the gym before work."

Six Tips for Stamina

Most CEOs, in my experience, believe that fitness, discipline, and nutrition are important to them. In order to put in the type of long hours that leadership requires, you too need to know how to deal with stress. To do that, and so much more, here are six handy tips:

1. *Focus on wellness.* Believe it or not, many women I talk to have gone years without so much as a single wellness checkup. Particularly as we age, women need to go to the doctor more

often, not less. Start with a simple checkup, then get into the habit of regular checkups as well as simple diagnostics that can help measure and regulate your blood pressure, cholesterol, nutrition, weight, and even energy.

2. *Move your body.* Bar none, the first, middle, and last thing you can do to increase your stamina—which is like fuel for your journey from competence to confidence—is simply to move more, and more often. Moving isn't just for your body; it's for your mind as well. Physical activity releases endorphins, the "feel good" substances in our bodies, making us happier as a result. When we feel better, we do better, and the best way to feel better is to begin moving regularly before, during, and after work.

3. *Delegate.* Believe it or not, one of the things we hear women say is that they have a hard time finding the energy to do all they need to do simply because they have so much on their plates! To take more off your plate, spread the wealth around and delegate some of those chores that you don't necessarily have to do yourself.

4. *Practice self-care.* You can't appear confident, let alone have stamina, if you're not doing some type of self-care every single day. Do what works for you, what relaxes you, and what prepares you for your journey. Take a walk, take a sauna, take a bath, see a movie, go to a concert, read a book, take a class, or go on a date or long weekend—but make self-care as much of a priority in your personal life as self-preservation is in your professional life. You simply can't do one without the other. As Jennifer Dieas says, "You need to nourish your body just as much as you're nourishing your business. So one of my routines is to make sure that I always have really good healthy snacks at my home and at work for myself and for my staff because it's really important. We're dealing with people in such a high-touch kind of way every day that you want to make sure that you're think-ing clearly, because we're basically, you know, offering advice and guidance to the people who need it." Jennifer adds, "Any-thing physical that you can do to make sure you reduce the amount of stress that's in your body, whether it's yoga or run-ning or fitness classes, anything that you can do to get those stress hormones out is amazing."

5. *Join a team*. If self-care is difficult for you, enlist the help of a few close, trusted friends or coworkers to join together as you all learn to take care of one another. We can't make it alone in this life. Trust me, I've tried. We need others to make life complete, but also to make life better. The more we share with others, the more we learn about ourselves. And when you surround yourself with happy, friendly, positive people, you will find yourself more energized to face the task(s) at hand.

6. *Enjoy yourself*. I think a big part of stamina is having fun. I'm serious. Working with fun people, having a pleasant work environment, learning to laugh at—and with—yourself and oth-ers immediately lowers your stress and allows you to feel better, longer, increasing your stamina while you are having fun!

As women, we often put everyone else first: on the job, at home, and everywhere in between. Until we learn to practice self-care, stamina will always be an issue for us. But remember, you can't be all you need to be for everyone in your life if you don't take care of yourself first.

The Takeaway

Even sprinters have to train for weeks and months at a time, even if it's just for a short burst that takes less than a minute to run. Leaders are no different from athletes. If we want to complete the journey from competence to confidence and perform at the highest level, we must prepare accordingly and take pains to stay in good health, emotionally and physically, to ensure that we're able to maintain high energy and performance day in, day out, time and time again.

Too many of us try to shine so brightly, so often, that we burn out before we reach our peak potential. Settle in for the long haul and rise to the occasion when needed, but do your best to separate work and life so that you have the balance you need for an entire career, not just a "job."

18

Taking Control of Your Career

Finally, nothing requires more resilience than navigating a career that can span decades—and must weather the storm of countless setbacks, obstacles, challenges, and outright roadblocks. This chapter looks at the long term and provides sound strategies for creating habits that, if begun now, can ensure smooth sailing as you navigate your career and your journey from competence to confidence.

Planning for Potential

I think that very often, women don't necessarily plan their careers. We have a penchant to feel lucky if we get a job, let alone a promotion, and simply "wing it" from opportunity to opportunity until we find ourselves in some position that wasn't necessarily achieved by some grand design.

Case in point: Recently, I was talking to a client who wanted to be the chief HR officer for her company. Rather than just want it, she had actually studied the career trajectories, duties, and success habits of other chief HROs to become clear on what she'd need to be successful in that role. I was impressed by her "background investigation" into her dream job and immediately thought to myself that this person would get there because she had her career road map carefully and thoroughly planned out.

On the other hand, my transition into HR was by default. I ended up getting into the HR industry because at the beginning of my career, someone in leadership at the company I was working for asked if anyone had read the employee handbook.

Now, as someone who'd gone to Catholic school, I had been trained to read manuals when they were given to me. Therefore, I had in fact read the employee handbook! So my new career trajectory began the moment I told my boss "Yes, I've read it."

Suddenly, just because I raised my hand and said "yes," I was given an opportunity to work in the HR department of a major organization, which went on for a little while. I enjoyed HR, but it wasn't until later in my career that I began to form specific goals for myself.

Now, I never wanted to be the COO/CEO of a large corporation, but I knew that one day I wanted to have my own business that specialized in leadership for women. So I built a network, worked diligently, and positioned myself as I moved into the space I currently occupy.

That said, I personally challenge future leaders to know what their long-term plans are. Notice I said "their" long-term plans, not the plans that the team or friends or family or spouses think are appropriate. Know yourself, know your goals, know your desires and passion, and make that the target of your goals and plans moving forward. It doesn't have to be the "top." It's okay to say you want to be a VP or senior VP as opposed to the CEO of a large corporation. Whatever the ultimate goal, know what will be expected of you in that position. Just like my client who thoroughly researched the job description and unwritten expectations of being head of HR, know the ins and outs of what you're shooting for to make sure that you're fully equipped once your goal is met.

Five Steps for Setting Quality Career Goals

Setting goals is one thing, but reaching them is another. To ensure that you are sufficiently prepared to successfully navigate the career you actually want, here are five steps for setting quality career goals:

1. *Have a strategy, not just a plan.* The more strategically you can plan, the more proficiently you can prepare. For instance, today's companies want their leaders to have more global experience. Knowing this ahead of time, you can tailor your activities, opportunities, and credentials by casting a wider net and taking any and all international opportunities that arise in your current and future positions. Barring those, you can seek mentorship opportunities or take classes or seminars to increase the amount of globalization in your professional portfolio.

2. *Keep learning—stay curious.* Knowing the requirements of your "dream job," you can better ascertain if you have the right credentials to get it. Ask yourself: "Do I have the right degree, training, and experience for what I want to do?" If not, what should you do? Take training and courses to get the skills you'll need? Figure this out ahead of time and your goals will be easier to obtain.

3. *Invest in yourself.* As I suggested in the previous tip, sometimes you need to be willing to invest in yourself in the form of classwork, training, magazine and web subscriptions, books and seminars, online learning, etc. (You may also need to invest in appropriate business attire.) All this may involve you asking for development, training, and even certification in certain courses and taking advantage of a tuition reimbursement plan if your employer offers one. If not, pace yourself and make the financial investment on your own.

4. *Chart your progress.* Be sure to measure your progress so that you know where you are on your career trajectory. When we have a plan in place, it's critical to continually measure and reassess to ensure that our goals are current. You may be ahead of your timeline, or behind it. You may have achieved certain goals and forgotten to mark or measure them. By continually "checking in" to mark your progress, you can assess where you've been, where you are . . . and where you need to be.

5. *Bounce!* We learned in an earlier chapter how to bounce when challenges, setbacks, or obstacles litter our path. On that note, don't be afraid to change course, even midstream, if the right opportunity presents itself. Leadership changes, our priorities change, teams dissolve or members are reassigned, and we often find ourselves at a point far afield from where we thought we wanted to be. You may learn more about the role you thought you wanted and realize, halfway there, that what you actually want is just a little bit closer to another place or direction. That's fine. We call that growth, evolution, and progress, and it's what resilience—and this chapter—is all about.

In addition to those five steps, here is an important thing to remember about navigating your career: Time will pass whether or not you do anything about your career.

There is a great story of a woman who graduated from law school when she was 85 years old. After her story appeared in the press, people came up and said to her, "Oh my God, who is going to hire you at 85?" She replied that it did not matter because she was going to be 85 anyway *but now she had a law degree.*

The truth is that time passes. Yesterday has passed, today will pass, and, if we're lucky, tomorrow will pass, too. What matters is how you use that time strategically to make or break you as a leader.

We must be conscious of the passing of time and use it, thoughtfully, to our advantage. Too many of us take time for granted. We never move forward, only side-to-side—or even backward. If you let life push you around with no action plan for moving forward in a strategic, thoughtful, or purposeful way, you'll never get to your desired destination.

One thing I have observed from women over 40 is that, suddenly, they begin to wonder how they got where they are. I often hear them say, "This is not the life I had planned for myself." But I wonder: Did they have any plan at all? I tend to think that we are not as intentional about our lives and where we are going as we think we are, or ought to be. And so this is an invitation to create that intention—a place to create a road map for your life.

The Takeaway

Remember, it's *your* journey from competence to confidence. It's *your* career. Your career is *your* responsibility, not your company's and not anyone else's. It's important to concentrate your energy on what *you* want and not what anybody else can provide for you.

We take control of our careers by setting goals, focusing on a particular direction, taking feedback, and being open to that feedback. Charting, and changing, your course means that you may need to shift some of your behaviors and be willing to learn new ways of doing things you thought you had already covered.

Navigating your career from competence to confidence is as much about changing directions as it is about following a straight, linear path. Being willing to develop yourself as you progress in your company sends a strong signal about your potential for leadership. Just because your company won't pay to develop you doesn't mean that you shouldn't take a course here or there anyway. Take accountability for yourself and your own actions!

Investing in yourself doesn't have to break the bank. For just $25 you can attend a professional association meeting where you'll get to hear a great speaker who may actively change your life. I am so inspired by others that I never miss an opportunity to hear someone new speak, because I know that, at the very least, I'm going to hear a new perspective on some aspect of my career that I might be taking for granted.

I could go on, but the point here is this: You are the CEO of your own career, and the kinds of things that we do in terms of preparing ourselves for that make all the difference, not only in how we lead but for which organization.

Conclusion

At Half The Sky, and in this book, I talk about the "click"—
that place where your confidence and competence connect
so powerfully you can feel it.

And once you've felt that click, you will be able to do all of
those things we've talked about in this book, including:

o *Step up* to new opportunities. As Natalye Paquin says,
"Confidence is built over time, after you have experienced success. And the foundation of success is being prepared, knowing
your environment, asking for help, having the courtesy of trust
and respect, and once you get all the foundational stuff and you
experience success, it builds confidence."

o *Show up* with authority and expertise. According to Jennifer Dieas, "Know your material; do your research. If you're so well versed in what you're doing, so educated in what you're doing, nothing will really rattle you, and when it's your time, you can speak up when the conversation opens for you to be able to kind of interject, and it's that cool, calm demeanor that will really get you very far."

o *Suit up* in a way that makes a professional and personal impression. When it comes to femininity, Natalie Nixon says, "I traveled a lot throughout Asia. One of the things I really learned from Asian women who were executives and leaders at the company where I worked: they led with their femininity. And the reason why this stood out to me was because I realized American women do not do that. American women, I think, probably wrongly have thought that the way to be accepted at the table with the big boys is to act like a dude or to kind of like dampen or cloak what's feminine about us. But I think what we've missed is that there's extreme power in femininity."

o *Speak up* and say what you mean. Find your voice and your power. Stop waiting for everything to be perfect before you speak up and state your case. Be willing to say what you think and then watch and listen for the reactions in the room. Use your voice in a powerful way and begin to build your confidence by practicing the skill or presenting to small and large groups. Susan Jin Davis, SVP at Comcast, says, "Open your mouth. Speak up, for the love of God. Ask yourself: do you want to be in the race? If you do, look around at the men speaking up all the time. If you want to compete with them, get in there. Then think of it this way. You're in a race to the finish. The men get to start the race way ahead of you just because they're men. If you want to win, what are you going to do? Let them win or run the hell out of the race and compete? Get your game on and speak up."

o *Stop apologizing* for yourself. Don't make apologies for whatever perceptions folks might have felt about you in the past. Start fresh with a clean slate. Dawn Callahan explains, "I think that, ultimately, this lack of confidence comes from still wanting to put the power in somebody else's hands and say, 'I'm going to measure my value based on what you think of me.' And when you finally take that back and say, 'It doesn't really matter what you think of me,' then I think you get to this place of confidence." Don't say you are sorry just for being in the room.

o *Start now* where you are. Now's the time. There is no better time to start working on your confidence than this very moment. Straighten up and begin to put together the pieces you need to exude confidence, both personally and professionally. The only thing you can do wrong here is to fail to start. You've got this!

It's not an instant shift, but one that inevitably gives you the tools you'll need to succeed on your own schedule, on your own merit, even on your own terms. I don't call these skills a magic bullet, but they're certainly what I call a "toolkit for success."

So maybe you don't go from being a wallflower to an extrovert overnight, but you know that you have the right to—and the tools to—do just that if you so desire. This is why I say confidence and competence feed each other.

When you are confident, it helps you build skills to gain competence, and when you are competent, it gives you the expertise to feel confident. Thus empowered, you can feel freer to take charge of your own career.

But don't go it alone! Now that this book is coming to its end, I'm hoping that our time together is just beginning. Please feel free to visit and engage with me on social media—on Facebook, Twitter, LinkedIn, and my website—and drop me a line about how your own success journey is going. I look forward to hearing from you. And remember, confidence is not a magical notion or idea that only the chosen few possess. It is for you, too—you just have to tap into it and make it your own!

Hopefully, by now you have seen that, with focus, with a willingness to make changes, and by working on the four powerful traits I've exposed you to in this book—Relationships, Reputation, Results, and Resilience—you too can experience *The Confidence Effect*.

Index

About the Author

Grace Killelea is the CEO and Founder of The GKC Group, a leadership development company. The company launched its program for high-potential women in early 2013. Called Half The Sky Leadership Institute, it is dedicated to expanding opportunities for women leaders to advance and thrive. A second program—Quattro—launched in Fall of 2015, offers development for both men and women, with a co-ed platform. The GKC Group also offers executive coaching and consulting.

A veteran human resources and talent executive, Grace's career spanned 35 years in the retail and telecommunications industries. She served as Senior Vice President of Talent at Comcast Cable Corporation before retiring to launch Grace Killelea Consulting in 2012. Her work rests on what she has identified as the four cornerstones of leadership: relationships, reputation, results, and resilience. Using these pillars, CEOs, executives, and professionals elevate their leadership and transcend their perceived limitations to achieve sustained business and personal success. Whether she's captivating audiences or coaching one-on-one, Grace's leadership inspires change.

Grace is a strong advocate for personal and professional development opportunities, especially for women and minorities, and her influence extends to volunteer work as well. For over a dozen years, she was the national facilitator for a selective nine-month, intensive leadership curriculum for women in the telecommunications industry. Grace has worked with and mentored over 1,000 executive women leaders. A highly sought-after speaker, she is often the featured speaker at events that support women and girls. Grace also serves on the board of the Girl Scouts of Eastern Pennsylvania, and she is an avid fundraiser for organizations supporting research against breast and ovarian cancer.

Grace earned her master's degree in Human Resources from American University's Kogod School of Business and Public Affairs, where she graduated with honors. She is pursuing her doctorate in Business Administration with a concentration in Leadership. She is a certified Birkman Consultant and also trained at the prestigious Center for Creative Leadership in Greensboro, North Carolina, considered to be one of the best leadership programs in the United States. Grace resides in Philadelphia with her husband Leonard.

Connect with Grace Killelea:

Facebook: Grace Killelea and The Confidence Effect
Twitter: @gracekillelea
LinkedIn: www.linkedin.com/in/gracekillelea
Website: www.thegkcgroup.com